CUBAN
COCKTAILS

CUBAN
COCKTAILS

100 CLASSIC & MODERN DRINKS

RAVI DEROSSI, JANE DANGER & ALLA LAPUSHCHIK

PHOTOGRAPHY BY GABI PORTER

STERLING EPICURE
New York

STERLING EPICURE
New York

An Imprint of Sterling Publishing
1166 Avenue of the Americas
New York, NY 10036

Distributed in Canada by Sterling Publishing
c/o Canadian Manda Group, 664 Annette Street
Toronto, Ontario, M6S 2C8, Canada
Distributed in the United Kingdom by GMC Distribution Services
Castle Place, 166 High Street, Lewes, East Sussex, BN7 1XU, England
Distributed in Australia by Capricorn Link (Australia) Pty. Ltd.
P.O. Box 704, Windsor, NSW 2756, Australia

For information about custom editions, special sales, and premium and
corporate purchases, please contact Sterling Special Sales at
800-805-5489 or specialsales@sterlingpublishing.com.

Manufactured in Canada

2 4 6 8 10 9 7 5 3 1

www.sterlingpublishing.com

Some of the recipes in this book contain raw eggs. Consuming raw
or undercooked eggs may increase your risk of food-borne illness.
The young, elderly, pregnant women, and anyone who may be
immunocompromised should not consume them.

¡BIENVENIDOS
A CIENFUEGOS,
BIENVENIDOS
A CUBA!

CONTENTS

THE BAR & THE COUNTRY

"All roads lead to rum."

—W. C. FIELDS

CIENFUEGOS IS MANY THINGS: a hundred fires, a province, a breezy port city, a governor, a battle, a revolutionary, and a tropical gathering place in the pulsing heart of Manhattan's East Village.

Cienfuegos, Cuba—on the southern coast, facing the Cayman Islands—was founded on April 22, 1819, as Fernandina de Jagua by French emigrants led by Louis de Clouet and named in honor of the Spanish king, Fernando VII. When the settlement became a town a decade later, the king authorized changing its name to Cienfuegos to honor José Cienfuegos y Jovellanos, captain general of the island. As the nineteenth century progressed, Cienfuegos became a vital port city, strategic for sugarcane and tobacco production. In sun-drenched streets bathed in tropical breezes, men ordered their rums by the finger, and women sipped exotic punches.

At the end of the 1800s, Cuba tried desperately to throw off the chains of centuries of Spanish rule. The three-year Cuban War of Independence began in 1895, and its final three months transformed what had been a regional struggle for freedom into an international conflict, pulling the United States into the hostilities and sparking the Spanish-American War. Two weeks after the start of that war, three American ships set out to sever key undersea telegraph cables connecting the island and others in the region. In the Battle of Cienfuegos, which took place on May 11, 1898, the American ships destroyed the cable house and cut two of the three targeted lines before escaping from advancing Spanish forces.

Half a century later, Cuba was chafing under the military dictatorship of Fulgencio Batista y Zaldívar. A scrappy young student named Camilo Cienfuegos y Gorriarán, harried by officials for his antigovernment politics, left the country and, after a stay in New York, headed to Mexico. There he met Fidel Castro Ruz, who was plotting to overthrow Batista. In November 1956, Cienfuegos joined Castro and eighty other revolutionaries aboard the *Granma*, which sailed from Tuxpan, Mexico, to Playa Las Coloradas, near Niquero. Cienfuegos and only a dozen or so of the others survived Batista's counterattack, but the invaders rallied, and Cienfuegos soon became one of the revolution's strategic leaders, rising to the rank of *comandante*. Batista fled Cuba on January 1, 1959, yielding power to Castro's forces. But Cienfuegos's prominence didn't last. In October of that year, his plane disappeared over the ocean, never to be found.

Cuba today represents a distillation of its incredible history. It's a mixing pot, influenced for both good and bad by the cycle of occupation and the struggle for independence. Today the waters of Cienfuegos Bay lap at the city's shores. Groves of mangoes line its outskirts. Horse-drawn carriages remain a respectable form of transportation. Time moves slowly, and history clings to the spectacular architecture. Each afternoon, the park at the tip of the city, called La Punta, fills with families and friends. People cool themselves in the waters off the rocky coastline or sit leisurely around a bottle of Havana Club.

Rum, to the people of Cuba, is the spirit of fire. When we opened Cienfuegos in 2006, we wanted to capture some of that mysterious Cuban essence in a bright, cheerful, welcoming refuge from the harsh frenzy of New York City. On the corner of 6th Street and Avenue A in the East Village, tucked away on the second floor, you'll find Cienfuegos, the bar inspired by the spirit of Cuba. In this intimate space of faded pinks, greens, and yellows, the plaster cracks as if in some old house in Cuba. Each night, we light one hundred candles, one hundred fires, to embrace the past and present of rum culture and the community it inspires. Cienfuegos stands as an altar to the spirit of fire and our homage to Cuba. It has brought three of our greatest passions together here for you: hospitality, writing, and of course drinking. Our cocktails have a strong foundation in the classics, which we update into our modern interpretations. You will find both in the pages of this book.

We can't gather around a bottle of Havana Club yet, but we can capture that sense of community by gathering around the punch bowl, which predates the modern cocktail and represents centuries of history mixed together, transforming over time as palates and environments changed. After all, gathering around the punch bowl is a tradition as old as rum itself, and it played a part in another, earlier revolution in the Americas. Boston's Museum of Fine Arts houses the punch bowl that Paul Revere made to honor the Glorious 92, Massachusetts legislators who refused to obey the British Crown. Punch also made and unmade legendary pirates, including Bartholomew Roberts, the most successful raider of the golden age of piracy.

Unlike in America, Cuban cocktail culture never dissolved into a dark age of convenience aimed at easier, faster, sweeter intoxication. Prohibition, that thirteen-year failed experiment, inversely fortified cocktail culture in Cuba, creating its own golden age. Even today, Cuban cocktail menus prominently feature classics that barely see the light of day on menus stateside. Bartenders there have been organized as a group since 1924. At Café Madrigal, the bartender showed us his copy of the cocktail manual, which features 1,100 recipes, each footnoted with the history of the drink.

Trader Vic, a leading founder of the tiki style of cocktails, found that same respect when he visited the island in the 1930s. The skill and grace of the bartenders amazed him, and their knowledge inspired him (and, later, us). Bartenders accommodated customers' palates without sacrificing the integrity of the drinks—exactly what we try to do in New York City, gently guiding unwary customers away from Tequila Sunrises or Long Island Iced Teas while still giving them something they will enjoy.

For decades, Cuban bartenders have practiced their craft within the confines of the broader political and economic circumstances. In this regard, America's renewed relationship with Cuba offers much promise, and it's exciting to think what mixologists there will be able to create without such limitations. We can't wait to see what the future brings.

Miami

Key West

Marianao Havana Matanzas Cárdenas

Cienfuegos

Niquero Santiago de Cuba

Siboney Daiquirí Guantánamo Bay

N
W E
S

An exact PLAN of the
CITY, Fortifications & Harbour of
HAVANA
in the Island of CUBA.
From an Original Drawing taken on the Spot.

Universal Magazine. J. Hinton,
Newgate Street.

TIMELINE

★

Christopher Columbus claims Cuba for Spain.	**1492**
1514	Diego Velázquez de Cuéllar, Cuba's first governor, founds Havana.
1862	Facundo Bacardí y Massó founds his eponymous distillery in Santiago de Cuba.
Cuba's Ten Years' War with Spain for independence ends unsuccessfully.	**1878**
1895	The three-year Cuban War of Independence begins.
The USS *Maine* explodes in Havana Harbor, triggering the Spanish-American War. After Spain loses, it cedes control of Cuba to the United States.	**1898**
1902	Cuba becomes an independent republic, but America pressures the country to adopt the Platt Amendment, which allows the United States to intervene in Cuban affairs.
America reoccupies Cuba.	**1906**
1909	Cuba regains its independence.
1933	Fulgencio Batista leads the Sergeants' Revolt, a military coup that ousts the president.
America forgoes its legal right to interfere in Cuban affairs.	**1934**
1943	The USSR opens its embassy in Havana.
Fidel Castro and his army of guerrilla fighters, including his brother, Raúl, and Ernesto "Che" Guevara, oust Batista.	**1959**
1960	Castro nationalizes all American businesses in Cuba without compensation.
America breaks diplomatic ties with Cuba and sponsors the Bay of Pigs invasion, which fails. Cuba becomes a Communist nation.	**1961**
1962	The Soviet Union moves nuclear weapons to Cuba, triggering the Cuban missile crisis, which ends when America withdraws nuclear missiles from Turkey.
1999	A boat carrying Cuban refugees capsizes in the Straits of Florida. Five-year-old Elián González survives and is rescued, triggering a legal battle between his father, who calls for his son's return to Cuba, and his late mother's relatives in Florida, who petition the American government to grant the boy asylum.
Federal officials seize González and reunite him with his father in Cuba.	**2000**
2002	Prisoners seized during the war in Afghanistan and suspected of being al-Qaeda affiliates are taken to the U.S. naval base at Guantánamo Bay for interrogation.
Castro announces his retirement. Days later, his brother, Raúl, becomes president.	**2008**
2014	President Barack Obama and President Raúl Castro announce plans to restore diplomatic relations between the two countries.
America eases trade and travel restrictions on Cuba, and each reopens its embassy in the other's capital.	**2015**

★

IT'S A MAD DASH ACROSS MIAMI INTERNATIONAL AIRPORT to Terminal F, where most charter flights leave for Havana. But we aren't going to Havana. We're going to Cienfuegos. Our stated destination wins a series of confused looks from airport employees, which makes sense once we arrive: Just one flight per day lands on the one runway of Jaime González Airport. Head due south from Miami, and you're there. The plane is full of elderly American tourists on state-approved tours, Cubans going home, and us. Customs officials snap our photos, stamp our passports, and there we are.

We come through customs last, emerging from the airport into the bright Cuban sun. The car rental office lies behind a mango tree. The heavy, ripe fruits fall as we wait our turn on plush leather sofas. We get the keys to a brand-new Kia, not a '57 Chevy as we had hoped.

Cienfuegos is *la perla de sud*, the pearl of the South, a sleepy resort town of 150,000 people, famous for singer, musician, and bandleader Beny Moré … and not a lot else. The main square, Parque José Martí, has its own triumphal arch (page 142), smaller than the one in Place Charles de Gaulle in Paris and the one in Washington Square Park in Manhattan. We amble down the main thoroughfare,

weaving through people lined up at an ice cream shop. We have lunch at a *paladar*, the Spanish word for "palate," but in Cuba it refers to a family-owned and family-operated restaurant. The owner of the Los Lobos paladar has a strong affinity for rock music. A framed Ozzy Osbourne watches as we drink a couple of Cristal beers. The chef peers out to see if we're enjoying our chicken *cordon bleu*, a house specialty. On the roof of the Palacio de Valle, we find the first signs of Cuban cocktail culture—aside from our hotel's sad rum and coke, no limes available. The Palacio's rooftop bar features a full cocktail menu and two neatly dressed bartenders. We slowly sip a Ron Collins and Havana Special in the glorious afternoon sun.

Not far off, we spy the tip of La Punta, the dagger of land that juts into Cienfuegos Bay. Everyone seems to be heading there, so we follow. At the tip lies a park with a bar, and the *cantinero* (bartender) claims to make the best mojito. We take him up on his offer, and it's damn good. But fresh limes, we discover, are either hard to find or maybe not highly valued. It feels like half the city is here in the park, though, swimming and running around. A group of teenagers huddles around a bottle of Havana Club with plastic cups. There's a fish roast later that night if we're interested.

Heading back through the city, we come upon a small basement bar. The *cantinero*, Manny, wears a giant gold chain with a dollar sign pendant. We still haven't had a daiquirí, so we make amends. Manny announces that he's going to make it special for us and produces a fantastic Chivas daiquirí. Havana Club—the Cuban rum so special that American bartenders try to smuggle it out when they leave the country—is the norm for Manny. Chivas, the blended Scotch that our parents served when they had company, is more special here. But Manny's daiquirí is delicious. He proudly shows us the wine cellar and is shocked to learn that two of us are *cantineras*—female bartenders. Nevertheless, he likes the look of our daiquirí when we show him a picture.

All roads lead to Havana. That's what you have to remember when lost and driving though an area with more horse carts than cars. Before this trip, we didn't know that horses could give dirty looks—until we accidentally blocked one with our Kia. All roads may lead to Havana, but before you arrive the Policía will pull you over. Maybe the horse told the officers to watch out for us. They pull us over and check the rental agreement, our driver's licenses, and the trunk of the car. They seem mildly amused either by our plan to drive to Havana or by the panic in our eyes when it looks like this road might lead to a Cienfuegos jail cell. They tell us that we are "very pretty girls" and to "be careful."

The wide-open road to Havana is in better shape than most in Brooklyn, and, better yet, no horses. Fields of sugarcane line the highway. The cows look painfully skinny. A couple of guys flirt with us from their car. A few hours later, Havana appears in the distance.

But some of the most confusing road signs we've ever had to decipher thwart our arrival. Once again, we're lost. Even on the outskirts, Havana doesn't have the same resort-town sleepiness of Cienfuegos. It feels like we're in the Bronx trying to find our way to Times Square. We're in the right city but a world away. It turns out that we're in Guanabacoa, in the eastern part of the capital, an area famous for the Afro-Cuban religion Santería. A few lefts and a few rights, and signs for Habana Vieja, the old part of town, come into view. To make sure we're reading the signs right, we circle the roundabout one more time. That's the joy of a roundabout: You don't have to make a decision until you're ready.

As we get closer, the streets narrow, and we enter an old, worn postcard. The gorgeous buildings are falling apart. Colorful walls crumble, exposing dark substructures. Laundry hangs from windows. The dome of the National Capitol Building—El Capitolio, which housed the Cuban Congress and now contains the Cuban Academy of Sciences—rises above us. We pull over to orient ourselves on the map. The driver of a bike taxi pulls up alongside, says "No Mafia," and asks if we need help. He circles around the car and shows us where we are. Up two blocks, make a right, take it to the end, and that's the Malecón, the broad roadway, esplanade, and seawall that stretches from Havana Harbor to the Vedado district, where we're staying. It's our final road to Havana.

Since the recent economic reforms, a plethora of paladars have transformed some city streets into restaurant rows. People holding menus throw themselves at you. The air smells of gasoline. Heavy black smoke pours from the '57 Chevys and the Soviet-era Ladas.

During dinner at Café Laurent, we sip Havana Club Ritual and Ron Santiago 11 Year. The daiquirí here is pretty, but it's still missing the lime juice. The real cocktails come at Café Madrigal.

Owned and operated by film director Rafael Rosales, Café Madrigal is the first outpost of real Cuban cocktails that we find. Fresh lemon juice mixes with honey for a delicious Canchanchara. (See our version, the Honeysuckle, on page 132.) The bartender, Ricardo, shows us his bar book, *Cocteles Cubanos*, which explains the history of the Canchanchara. Then he gives us his recipe for the Mai Tai. A political science professor from St. Louis, who now lives in Cuba, plays the mandolin alongside the college-age guitar player at the microphone. We end the night with a round of tequila shots, just like at home.

Havana is city of historic bars. As often happens, historic bars die in time, stunted by the moment that made them matter in the first place. El Floridita seethes with tourists who snap pictures next to the Hemingway statue. Papa Doble is good, but nothing about the space makes you want to sit awhile. Sloppy Joe's looks like any other American bar. The vibrant center of living history is Bodeguita del Medio. Signatures of prior customers cover every inch of the place. Bartender Arturo is as old-school as they come, as quick with a light for a cigar as he is with a drink. The mojitos are good, too. We sign our names on barstools, listen to the band, and drink our mojitos.

At that moment, Havana feels perfect.

THE REQUIREMENTS

& THE METHODS

These are the basic tools, ingredients,
and techniques you'll need to make
the perfect drink every time.

A   B   C   D

BARWARE

"It's my industrial-strength hair-dryer, and I can't live without it!" says Princess Vespa in *Spaceballs*. Cocktail enthusiasts and experts alike cling to specific tools that fit their style of bartending. What works and makes sense for one person might seem like complete insanity to another. With a little experimentation, you can identify your own industrial-strength hair-dryers.

BARSPOONS

These long-handled spoons used for stirring sometimes feature a twisted shaft. The barspoon also serves as a measurement—except there's no uniform size for a barspoon. Using the same barspoon for all barspoon measurements will ensure consistency. **A**

BLENDER

For preparing frozen drinks, the blender should have a strong motor capable of crushing ice easily. For blending liquid ingredients, a stick or immersion blender is fine, but use a countertop model for ice. **B**

GRATER

Use a handheld grater just as you would for preparing food. **C**

JIGGER

A jigger is absolutely integral to measuring consistent, quality drinks. A one- and two-ounce jigger and a ½- and ¾-ounce jigger will cover all bases. Taller, Japanese-style jiggers feature interior markings for smaller measures. **D**

  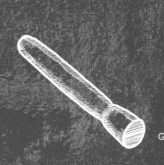 

JUICER

Whether you use an electric juicer or a handheld model, fresh juice is absolutely essential for good cocktails. **E**

MIXING GLASS

From a pint glass to Japanese cut crystal, mixing glasses come in all shapes and sizes, but glass is key to control dilution. A metal shaker can work in a pinch, but makes it harder to chill the drink without overdiluting it. **F**

MUDDLER

This large stick will release the flavor of herbs and fruit or beat someone up—depending on your agenda. Wooden muddlers can be high maintenance, and textured ones can prove too aggressive on delicate ingredients. Look for one that's smooth and heavy. **G**

SHAKERS

We prefer the weighted shaker, in which an 18-ounce metal shaker fits into a 28-ounce shaker. This workhorse style is most common behind the bar.

Other styles include the Parisian shaker, the cobbler, and the Boston shaker. In the Parisian, two stainless steel tins join with a clean seam that may or may not be secure. Use a two-hand shake to be sure. After the Parisian came the cobbler, which features a cap that goes over the strainer portion of the tin, which fits into the larger bottom tin. The cobbler is elegant and does the job well, but the top can prove difficult to remove, and the built-in strainer doesn't let you adjust the strain. The Boston shaker consists of a pint glass and a large shaking tin. Glass is the downside to the Boston shaker. It can't chill a drink as well as metal, and it instantly becomes a deadly weapon with the slightest slip. **H**

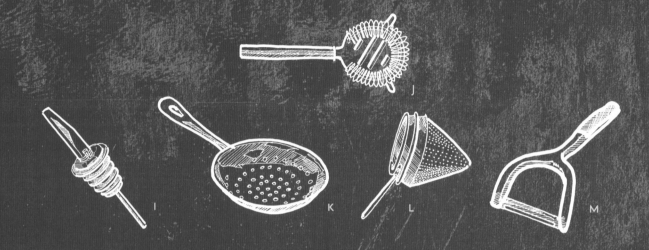

SPEED POURERS

These control the flow of liquid from the bottle, allowing you to measure accurately without spilling. Make sure the speed pourer fits into the bottle well to prevent wasting alcohol. I

STRAINERS

Flat-topped, perforated, and with a metal spiral around the perimeter, the Hawthorne strainer fits snugly into the large tin of an 18–28, Boston, or Parisian shaker. Push the Hawthorne strainer forward to adjust the straining level. Julep strainers, consisting of a shallow perforated bowl attached to a handle, are used to strain stirred drinks. They should fit snugly into your preferred mixing glass. The cone strainer is basically a small sieve that ensures that no ice chips or bits of muddled fruit or herbs escape the Hawthorne strainer and affect the texture of a drink. J, K, L

Y-SHAPED VEGETABLE PEELER

This kitchen tool is handy behind the bar for making twists. M

GLASSWARE

Besides using the right barware to make cocktails, it's equally important to use the appropriate serving vessels for them. Every container has its specific reason and purpose.

BEER GLASS

This pint glass (16 ounces) is either conical in shape or nonik ("no-Nick"), which bulges slightly toward the top.

COLLINS GLASS

Named after the Tom Collins cocktail, this tall, cylindrical glass holds 10 to 14 ounces. The highball glass is a shorter, wider variation.

COUPE

Reportedly modeled after Marie Antoinette's left breast, this timeless classic holds 5 to 6 ounces. Used for Champagne in the past, it has become the gold standard for serving craft cocktails. Chill them in advance.

FIZZ GLASS

This lovechild of a coupe and cocktail (martini) glass holds 6 to 8 ounces.

FLUTE

Concave, trumpet-shaped, or cylindrical but always narrow, to avoid surface-area loss of carbonation, a flute is always on a stem to prevent the drinker's hand from warming the drink. It holds 4 to 7 ounces.

MUG

A mug is a ceramic cup that holds 6 to 8 ounces and, like a teacup, features a handle for holding hot drinks. Glass variations usually are larger and narrower (to avoid heat loss) than punch glasses.

PUNCH BOWL

These large serving vessels, often though not exclusively glass or crystal, hold at least 64 ounces and come with matching ladles.

PUNCH GLASS

A small glass or crystal mug that holds 4 to 6 ounces.

ROCKS GLASS

A square or cylindrical glass that holds 8 ounces and has a thick base. A double rocks glass is the same shape but holds twice the volume.

SWIZZLE GLASS

A footed pilsner glass that holds 10 to 16 ounces.

TIKI BOWL

These stylized, sculptural, often ceramic vessels hold 16 to 20 ounces and come in various Pacific incarnations meant to represent Polynesian gods or spirits.

WINE GLASS

Generically a glass bowl that holds 4 to 8 ounces atop a glass stem and foot. Numerous variations allow for different volumes and surface areas and for cupping aromas or vapors.

INGREDIENTS

BITTERS

Once upon a time bitters were medicine, a blend of herbs and botanicals steeped in alcohol that served as a cure-all. We now use many of those same bitters to round out our cocktails. When a brand of bitters is specified, that specific bitter is integral to the drink. However, experimentation is an important part of the learning experience.

CARBONATION

For the recipes in the book, we've indicated using a dry sparkling wine. We prefer Gruet Brut. Add any carbonated or sparkling ingredients after you've poured the drink into the glass. Don't shake or mix afterward.

CITRUS

We can't emphasize the importance of fresh citrus juice enough. Desperation might have you reaching for the prepackaged or bottled stuff or, worse, something in a plastic squeeze bottle, but nothing ever beats the real thing. Think of citrus like dairy. You want it as close to the original as commercially possible. Anything else is a bad idea.

CREAM

Organic heavy cream is best for making cocktails.

EGGS

Eggs used in cocktails should be small, brown organic eggs. Note: Consuming raw or undercooked eggs may increase your risk of food-borne illness. For extra safety, bathe eggs quickly in water (90 to 120°F), then dry them immediately.

GARNISHES

Cherries for garnish should be brandied or candied, such as the Luxardo brand. No neon maraschino monsters, please!

Always rasp cinnamon, nutmeg, and other grated garnishes fresh to optimize their aromatics.

When muddling mint, use only the leaves—no stems—and reserve the best sprig tops for garnish. Tap the mint against the back of your hand to release the oils before garnishing.

Salt for rimming should be kosher rough salt. The texture is more conducive than table or other kinds of salt to cocktail preparation and drinking.

For twists, use a Y-shaped peeler on citrus fruit. Avoid the pith, which adds unwanted bitterness. Pinch the twist, skin side down, over the drink, rub it around the rim of the glass, then float it, skin side up, in the drink.

ICE

Water holds our bodies together as well as our drinks. Achieving proper dilution makes for a properly chilled and balanced drink. Good, solid ice helps you achieve that. When shaking a mixture over ice, use crushed ice. If you don't have crushed ice or a refrigerator that will dispense it, put a handful of ice cubes in a clean plastic bag, and crush them with a wooden mallet or meat tenderizer before putting them into the cocktail shaker.

If serving a drink on the rocks, always build the full drink first and add the ice last, immediately before serving.

PUREES

You can make your own at home if you prefer, but for the home bartender it's a lot of additional work with ingredients that might be hard to find. The goal is to use a puree that doesn't include added sugar. The brand we prefer is Perfect Puree, which you can find at any good specialty food store or online.

RUM

When colonists set sail from Western Europe in the sixteenth and seventeenth centuries, they discovered that the cash crop in the New World was sugar. (See below.) After gold and silver mines, the fortunes of the Western Hemisphere came from sugar fields. Processing sugarcane into sugar resulted in molasses. From molasses came a fiery, distilled spirit with an equally fiery name—"kill-devil" or rumbullion—which sailed up and down the Eastern Seaboard, fueling much of the New World's development. Rum once dominated these new dominions. But people still looked down on its rough edges. It was, after all, the by-product of a by-product.

Today rum is a complex, nuanced spirit, and its three main styles still hark back to centuries and colonies past. The English style is big and burly, found in Jamaica, Barbados, the Virgin Islands, and Trinidad and Tobago. The French style of Haiti, Martinique, and Guadeloupe uses mostly sugarcane to produce earthy, grassy, herbal *agricole* rums. The Spanish style, made in Cuba, Puerto Rico, Nicaragua, Guatemala, Panama, Venezuela, and the Dominican Republic, has a certain delicateness to it. Cachaça is a sugarcane-based spirit made predominantly in Brazil.

Whatever the style, rum is an extremely diverse category. When recipes in this book call for specific brands, rather than just a style, it's because the other ingredients work specifically with that brand. If you can't find that brand, you may have to refine your approach and make a few extra drinks—but that's all part of the fun.

SUGAR

Sugar is the paterfamilias of rum. Most of us already have white sugar on hand at home, so that one's easy.

Demerara, on the northern coast of South America, was a Dutch colony until 1815 and part of British Guiana until 1966. The sugar that bears its name originally came from cane fields there, but now it's a style rather than a designation of origin. To make demerara sugar, producers press sugarcane and steam the juice of the first pressing to form thick cane syrup. That's allowed to dehydrate, leaving behind large, golden-brown crystals of sugar. Because it's not refined, demerara sugar has a rich, creamy, molasses-like flavor.

Cane syrup is made from juice extracted from raw sugarcane stalks and boiled down until thick. It's much easier to buy than to make.

SYRUPS

Syrups are to cocktails what salt is to cooking. See the following section for more details.

VERMOUTH

Vermouth begins to appear in the mid-eighteenth century in Turin, Italy, the home of this wine fortified with neutral grape brandy. Traditionally there are two main styles: dry and sweet. Dry is often called French-style in old cocktail manuals, and sweet vermouth is often referred to as Italian. From sweet vermouth in the Manhattan to dry vermouth in the martini, the fortified wine plays a crucial role in many of America's oldest and most well-known cocktails.

In addition to those two styles, here are a few variations. Bianco vermouth is similar to dry vermouth but sweeter and with prominent vanilla notes. (A wonderful brand is Dolin Bianco, produced in Chambray, France.) Amber vermouth tastes similar to sweet vermouth but is lighter in color and sweetness. Noilly Prat Amber is a staple in this style, with strong notes of vanilla and cinnamon. Made of both rosé and white wine, rosé vermouth, a combination of the sweet and bianco styles, is citrus and vanilla forward.

SYRUPS & INFUSIONS

Syrups aren't just cloying sweeteners. They can improve a cocktail in many ways—adding unique flavors, providing body, and taming stubborn ingredients—that liquors and other modifiers can't. Infusions offer another method for expanding the creativity of a drink. Alcohol loves to be infused, soaking up and combining flavors with minimal effort, through simple maceration.

SIMPLE SYRUP

2 cups white sugar
2 cups water

Stir in a pan on low heat until they combine. Refrigerated, the mixture will last for three weeks.

AGAVE SYRUP

1 cup agave nectar
1 cup water

Build in pan, and stir over low heat until combined. It will keep in the refrigerator for two to three weeks.

BANANA RUM

1 750 ml bottle demerara 151 rum
3 very ripe bananas

In a large bowl, mash the bananas, and add the rum. Chill for 48 hours in the refrigerator, and then fine strain. This rum will keep indefinitely in your liquor cabinet.

CHILI SYRUP

10 medium red chilis
2 cups white sugar
2 cups water

Cut peppers lengthwise, and put in a pan with the sugar and water. Cook for 10 minutes over medium heat. Blend the peppers, and fine strain the mixture. It will keep in the refrigerator for two weeks.

CINNAMON SYRUP

10 cinnamon sticks
2 cups water
2 cups white sugar

Place all ingredients in a saucepan, bring to a boil, and turn off the heat. Cover, and let sit at room temperature for 24 hours. Strain out the cinnamon, and refrigerate. The syrup will keep for two weeks.

DEMERARA SYRUP

2 cups demerara sugar
2 cups water

Heat in a sauce pan on medium heat until sugar and water fully combine. The mixture will keep for three weeks in the refrigerator.

GINGER SYRUP

1 cup ginger juice
1 cup demerara sugar
    or brown sugar
1 cup white sugar

Build in a saucepan, and cook on low heat until the sugar dissolves. Cool, and refrigerate. The mixture will keep for two weeks.

GREEN TEA CACHAÇA

1 750 ml bottle cachaça
¾ cup green tea leaves

Stir together in large pitcher, let sit for 30 minutes, and strain leaves. It keeps indefinitely.

GRENADINE

2 cups pomegranate juice
1 cup white sugar
⅛ teaspoon rose water
peel of 1 large orange

Cook all ingredients over medium heat for 10 minutes. Strain out peel. The mixture will keep in the refrigerator for two or three weeks.

HONEY SYRUP

1 ½ cups honey
1 ½ cups water

Heat in a pan on low until combined. The syrup keeps in the refrigerator for three weeks.

HOT HONEY SYRUP

1 ½ cups honey
10 ounces water
2 ounces white rum
5 jalapeños

Combine honey and water and bring to a boil. Add the rum and jalapeños. Blend well, and fine strain. The mixture will keep for two weeks.

MINT SYRUP

2 cups white sugar
2 cups water
15 mint leaves

Heat sugar and water on low in a small pan until they combine.

Add the mint leaves, and let them steep for 30 minutes. Strain out the leaves, and the mixture will last in the refrigerator for three weeks.

ORGEAT

This is an essential almond-based syrup for many tiki drinks, though one of the first cocktails to use it wasn't a tiki drink but the Japanese Cocktail created by bartending forefather Jerry Thomas in honor of the first Japanese diplomatic mission to America in 1860. Pronounced "OR-zhah" in French or "OR-zhat" or "OR-zhee-uht" in English.

1 pound whole raw almonds
4 cups water
2 cups white sugar
1 cup demerara
   or light brown sugar
1 ounce cognac
¾ teaspoon orange flower water

Preheat oven to 350°F. In a food processor, chop the almonds medium to fine. Spread them on a baking sheet and cook for 12 to 15 minutes, until golden. In a deep pan, combine the water, the toasted almonds, and both sugars. Cook on medium heat until the mixture comes to a boil. Blend with an immersion blender or traditional blender into a thick paste. Fine strain by pressing through cheesecloth or a fine wire-mesh strainer. Add the cognac and orange flower water; stir well. Seal in a bottle or container, and the mixture will keep in the refrigerator for two weeks.

PASSION FRUIT SYRUP

2 cups passion fruit puree
2 cups white sugar

Build in a saucepan and cook on low heat, stirring until sugar fully combines. Remove from heat and let cool. Refrigerate. The syrup will last for two weeks.

RAISIN RUM

2 cups raisins
1 750 ml bottle Mount Gay rum

Place rum and raisins in a large container. Cover and let sit at room temperature for 24 hours. Strain, and save raisins for garnish or baking.

RHUBARB SYRUP

2 cups raw rhubarb, diced
2 cups white sugar
2 cups water

Build in pan, bring to a simmer over medium heat, and cook until rhubarb is soft, 10 to 12 minutes. Remove from heat and let cool. Press through fine strainer. The syrup will keep in the refrigerator for up to two weeks.

VANILLA SYRUP

2 vanilla pods
2 cups water
2 cups white sugar

Cut the vanilla pods lengthwise, and scrape out the seeds. Put the seeds, pods, water, and sugar in a small pan, and heat until the sugar combines. Let sit 24 hours at room temperature. Strain out the pods, and chill the liquid in the refrigerator. The mixture keeps for two weeks.

TECHNIQUES

Sometimes it really is the motion of the ocean. Here's how to do the job right.

BLEND

When using a countertop blender and cubed or crushed ice, pulse generously to break the ice without breaking the machine.

If using a stick blender, always keep the blades and their protective cover below the surface level of the liquid. Otherwise you'll be wearing your cocktail rather than drinking it.

CHILL

Put glassware in a freezer or fill it with an ice-water bath before mixing or shaking a drink. For hot drinks, do the opposite: Chafe the glassware first with hot water.

MIX

When building mixed drinks to be shaken or stirred, start with smaller volume and least expensive ingredients first: dashes of bitters, fruits or herbs to be muddled, juices, syrups, modifiers, and finally the base spirit. Recipe conventions list alcohols first, then non-alcohols, and both in descending order, but that's for planning rather than making. Now you know.

MUDDLE

The key is to press rather than smash. You want to coax the juices or oils from fruit or herbs rather than crushing them from them. The harder you push, the more likely you'll release bitterness from the plant structure rather than the botanical essence.

RIM

For cocktails requiring a sugar or salt rim, wipe a lemon or lime wedge around the edge of the glass. Then hold the glass upside down and roll the outside only in salt or sugar. Don't get any inside the glass or you'll radically alter the flavor profile of the drink.

SHAKE

Shaken drinks typically contain citrus, cream, eggs, fruit, or herbs. Depending on the size of the ice cubes, shaking time may vary, but shake like you mean it, hard and fast. Don't go crazy, though: no more than 8 to 12 seconds. Shaking for longer than that is showing off and risks bruising the drink. Your goal is to chill, dilute, and aerate the cocktail, not to agitate it to death.

Always make sure the tin is closed tightly. Cobbler shakers (page 3) have a built-in strainer, but we prefer weighted shaking tins.

When building drinks, prepare them in the smaller tin, reserving the larger one for eggs or cream. When making cocktails with eggs or cream, add them right before mixing to avoid curdling, and dry shake (no ice) for 5 to 7 seconds to emulsify. Then shake with ice for 10 to 15 seconds to chill and dilute.

Strain shaken drinks from the large half of the metal tin using a Hawthorne strainer.

Another method is the whip shake, by which you shake a drink with only one ice cube or a few pellets of crushed ice to incorporate the ingredients before straining.

STIR

Stirred cocktails consist primarily of spirits and modifiers. Prepare them in a mixing glass with plenty of ice to dilute and chill them. Cracking the ice will allow you to fit more in the glass to chill properly.

Pour stirred drinks from the mixing glass through a julep strainer into the serving vessel.

STRAIN

How you strain and which strainer you use depend on what kind of drink you're making.

THE SPIRIT

& THE COLONIAL

Stirred cocktails highlight the rich nuances of rum as a base spirit, while punches, flips, fizzes, and hot concoctions recall the colonial preferences for rum consumption.

STIRRED COCKTAILS

As defined in 1806, the original cocktail consisted of a spirit, sugar, bitters, and water. The next year, Frederic Tudor, "the Ice King," successfully delivered frozen water to Cuba. Sugar production had made rum flow, but the product was rough and lacking. The necessary improvement in quality came after the invention of the continuous column still in 1826 by Aeneas Coffey in Dublin, Ireland. His design allowed not only for the production of more spirit but a lighter one at that.

Around 1848, continuous stills began appearing in Cuba. Modern distilleries were emerging in Havana, Cárdenas, Matanzas, and Santiago de Cuba, but Cuban rums still fell below the estimation of their British and Spanish rivals. Then, in 1862, Facundo Bacardí y Massó pioneered a new style of rum, lighter and drier than the rough spirit that preceded it, by using a continuous still, charcoal filtration, and oak aging. His new process and shrewd marketing began a new era. Other brands, including Havana Club, Matusalem, and Camps, followed. In 1876, Bacardí entered his light rum in an international competition at the Philadelphia Centennial Exhibition and won the gold medal. Cuban rum officially had become the gold standard, quickly differentiating itself from the other players.

It was time to make some drinks.

COCKSPUR & BULL SPECIAL

In 1941, John Morgan, owner of the Cock 'n' Bull Restaurant on Sunset Boulevard in Los Angeles and a ginger beer company of the same name, John Martin, president of Heublein Spirits, and Rudolph Kunett, president of Heublein's Smirnoff division, invented the Moscow Mule at the Chatham Hotel on East 48th Street in Manhattan. Ten years later, a recipe for the Cock 'n' Bull Special, which uses bourbon as the base spirit, appeared in Ted Saucier's *Bottoms Up*, published in 1951. For the base of our Cuban-inspired variation, we substitute Cockspur Rum, first produced by a Dutch sailor named Valdemar Hanschell in 1884.

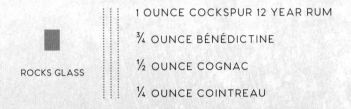

ROCKS GLASS

1 OUNCE COCKSPUR 12 YEAR RUM

¾ OUNCE BÉNÉDICTINE

½ OUNCE COGNAC

¼ OUNCE COINTREAU

Stir all ingredients over ice, and strain into a double rocks glass with big ice. Garnish optionally with an orange twist.

BETWEEN THE SHEETS

In the years before Prohibition, mixing base spirits together was thought to lead to sudden intoxication. Patrick Gavin Duffy—longtime bartender at the Ashland House Hotel in New York City and author of *The Official Mixer's Manual* (1934)—asterisked this cocktail, indicating that he didn't recommend it. Poet Edna St. Vincent Millay disagreed, however; this drink was said to be her favorite.

COUPE

1½ OUNCES APPLETON ESTATE V/X RUM

¾ OUNCE LOUIS ROYER FORCE 53 VSOP COGNAC

½ OUNCE COINTREAU

1 BARSPOON LEMON JUICE

1 DASH ANGOSTURA BITTERS

LEMON FOR GARNISH

Stir all ingredients over ice, then strain into a chilled coupe. Garnish with a lemon twist.

★ NOTE ★

The same year that Long & Smith published Duffy's Official Mixer's Manual, Harper issued Millay's Wine from These Grapes; in "Conscientious Objector," one of the poems in the book, Millay notes that Death has business in Cuba.

RUM OLD-FASHIONED

The ingredients of the Old-Fashioned first appeared together in print in 1806, earning the drink the distinction of being the first printed recipe for a cocktail. But in the 1870s, as cocktail culture developed and replaced the outdated drink with new libations, the first-born became known as the old-fashioned. For a long, dark period in the history of the Old-Fashioned, cherries, orange slices, club soda, and other nonsense bastardized it—a time that thankfully has passed. Our Rum Old-Fashioned takes inspiration from the granddaddy of cocktails but uses the nuances of rum as the base spirit.

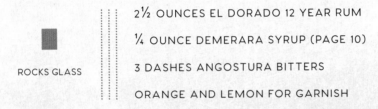

ROCKS GLASS

2½ OUNCES EL DORADO 12 YEAR RUM

¼ OUNCE DEMERARA SYRUP (PAGE 10)

3 DASHES ANGOSTURA BITTERS

ORANGE AND LEMON FOR GARNISH

Stir all ingredients over ice, and strain into a rocks glass with ice. Garnish with orange and lemon twist.

★ NOTE ★

As you will see throughout this book, rum has an uncanny ability to substitute for other spirits, providing compelling variations of classic cocktails. This recipe offers a prime example.

ISLAND LIGHTNING

Laird's Applejack is an apple brandy made by Laird & Company, the oldest licensed distillery in America. It sometimes goes by the name of Jersey Lightning, and during the colonial period it was used to pay road construction crews in what became the Garden State. Chairman's Reserve Spiced Rum has notes of cinnamon, clove, and nutmeg that partner especially well with the applejack.

PUNCH GLASS

1 OUNCE CHAIRMAN'S RESERVE SPICED RUM

¾ OUNCE LAIRD'S APPLEJACK

¼ OUNCE DEMERARA SYRUP (PAGE 10)

1 TEASPOON LEMON JUICE

2 DASHES PEYCHAUD'S BITTERS

ORANGE, APPLE, AND CINNAMON STICK FOR GARNISH

Stir all ingredients over ice, and strain into a punch glass. Twist an orange rind over the top to expel the oils, and discard. Garnish with an apple slice and a cinnamon stick.

★ NOTE ★

Robert Laird served in the Continental Army under George Washington, who once asked him for his recipe for "cyder spirits." Laird & Company received License No. 1 from the Treasury Department in 1780.

FAIR & WARMER

Based on the 1915 comic play of the same name by Avery Hopwood—one of the early twentieth century's successful but now largely forgotten playwrights—this cocktail first appeared in Hugo Ensslin's 1916 *Recipes for Mixed Drinks*. The success of the 1919 silent film adaptation of the play prompted repeat appearances of the cocktail in Harry Craddock's *Savoy Cocktail Book* (1930) and Patrick Gavin Duffy's *Official Mixer's Manual* (1934). It's a simple drink, but it clearly has staying power.

COUPE

1½ OUNCES FLOR DE CAÑA 7 YEAR RUM

1 OUNCE DOLIN ROUGE VERMOUTH

½ OUNCE COINTREAU

Stir all ingredients over ice, and strain into a chilled coupe.

★ NOTE ★

In the film version of Fair and Warmer, Billy the banker suspects his wife, Laura, of being unfaithful. When their upstairs neighbors, Jack and Blanny, come down to play cards, Jack reveals to Billy that he tells Blanny that he's going to the Mystic Shrine whenever he needs to account for his absence. Jack and Laura each leave independently, and Billy and Blanny discuss their mutual suspicions and get drunk. But it all ends happily, of course.

SINKING SPELL

Carthusian monks have been making Chartreuse liqueur in the mountains of the same name near Grenoble in the southeast of France since 1737, following instructions reportedly given to them in a secret manuscript more than a century earlier by François d'Estrées, a military officer. Green and yellow are the most common types, though aged and commemorative variations exist. The herbal notes of the Chartreuse are supported by the J. M. Blanc, one of a few rums that can make a claim to having terroir. The sugarcane used to produce J. M. Blanc grows in a unique microclimate of Martinique's Mount Pelée, which features volcanic soil and produces a rum that tastes of fresh sugarcane, ripe bananas, and mango with a hint of earthiness.

ROCKS GLASS

2 OUNCES J. M. BLANC RUM

½ OUNCE YELLOW CHARTREUSE

1 BARSPOON CANE SYRUP

2 DASHES ORANGE BITTERS

STAR ANISE FOR GARNISH

Stir all ingredients over ice, and strain into a rocks glass with ice. Garnish with a star anise.

★ NOTE ★

This cocktail, which acknowledges the French origins of the city of Cienfuegos, takes its name from the eponymous story by Edward Gorey.

CLUB COCKTAIL

The Club Cocktail is a variation on the Manhattan No. 1 from the *Savoy Cocktail Book*. It's called the Club Cocktail because it belongs to the club of Manhattan variations that span the spectrum of drinks from the Brooklyn to the Rob Roy. Our version, which of course uses rum instead of whiskey, is also similar to a perfect Manhattan. The play of dry vermouth and sweet vermouth is perfecto!

COUPE

2 OUNCES CHAIRMAN'S RESERVE SPICED RUM

½ OUNCE DOLIN DRY VERMOUTH

½ OUNCE DOLIN ROUGE VERMOUTH

1 DASH ANGOSTURA BITTERS

1 DASH MARASCHINO

BRANDIED CHERRY FOR GARNISH

Stir all ingredients over ice, and strain into a chilled coupe. Garnish with a brandied cherry.

★ NOTE ★

In the days before liquor production standards, spices helped make unaged or inferior rums palatable. Sailors used allspice, black pepper, cassia, cinnamon, cloves, ginger, mace, nutmeg, and other spices to cover and mellow the rums they drank.

EL PRESIDENTE

Several bars in Havana claim to have invented El Presidente, although David Wondrich points to American expat Eddie Woelke as its creator. The recipe first appeared in print in a newspaper in 1919, so the president in question would have been Mario García Menocal y Deop, second president of the second republic. Charles Baker called the drink the "Habana Presidente, now known to many, but sound enough in its own right for listing in any spiritual volume. This has long been one of Cuba's favorite drinks, and every visiting Americano should go to La Florida and get one."

COUPE

¾ OUNCE DOLIN BLANC VERMOUTH

¾ OUNCE EL DORADO 3 YEAR RUM

¾ OUNCE LA FAVORITE RHUM BLANC

¼ OUNCE CURAÇAO

1 BARSPOON GRENADINE (PAGE 10)

LEMON FOR GARNISH

Stir all ingredients over ice, and strain into a chilled coupe. Twist lemon rind over top, and discard.

> ★ NOTE ★
>
> *El Presidente was the house cocktail at Club El Chico in Manhattan's Greenwich Village, where America first encountered the rhumba in 1925. Turn the page for more information about the origin of the cocktail.*

LA HISTORIA
DEL PRESIDENTE

Prohibition in America prompted a lot of bartenders to head to the Caribbean. German-born Eddie Woelke was one of them. In New York City, he worked at the Hotel Knickerbocker and then the Biltmore Hotel. As Prohibition barreled forward, the owners of the Biltmore Hotel purchased the Hotel Sevilla in Havana, and Woelke migrated south to open the new Sevilla-Biltmore Hotel.

García Menocal y Deop attended the grand opening of the hotel, which in his honor served El Presidente, a combination of rum, French vermouth, and grenadine. Woelke didn't create El Presidente, but he did popularize it with his celebrity barman status. When Gerardo Machado y Morales (pictured left) became president of Cuba in 1925, Woelke modified El Presidente by adding Curaçao and renaming it Presidente Machado. Over time, Woelke's Presidente Machado has become the standard recipe for El Presidente.

PAN AMERICAN TRILOGY

Pan American Airways began its storied history by connecting Key West to Havana. The first flight, which carried air mail only, took place on October 19, 1927. Three months later, on January 16, 1928, seven passengers made the first commercial flight from Key West to Havana. Pan American soon became America's largest international airline, a distinction it held until 1991, but this cocktail celebrates its humble origins.

ROCKS GLASS

1 OUNCE DIPLOMATICO AÑEJO RUM

1 OUNCE LAIRD'S APPLE BRANDY

¼ OUNCE CINNAMON SYRUP (PAGE 10)

¼ OUNCE DEMERARA SYRUP (PAGE 10)

10 DROPS BITTERMENS TIKI BITTERS

1 DASH ABSINTHE

APPLE FOR GARNISH

Stir all ingredients over ice, and strain into a rocks glass with ice. Garnish with an apple slice.

★ NOTE ★

The drink takes its name from the American Trilogy, a cocktail offered at Little Branch in the West Village and created by Richie Bocatto and Michael Mcilroy. Here rye gives way to rum, cinnamon syrup replaces sugar, and absinthe makes an appearance—all to give an American classic more of a Cuban feel.

FIFTY-FIRST STATE

At the end of the Spanish-American War, America took hold of the last vestiges of the once vast Spanish Empire: Cuba, Puerto Rico, the Philippines, and Guam. But this wasn't the first time that the United States took a political interest in the area. After all, Caribbean molasses and rum had helped fuel the Revolutionary War. In 1917, Congress passed the Jones-Shafroth Act, which gave American citizenship to all eligible Puerto Ricans. (The Puerto Rican House of Delegates, which saw the law as a way to draft more men into the U.S. Army for America's imminent role in World War I, unanimously opposed it.) This cocktail was created in honor of Puerto Rico's 2012 referendum on territorial status, the first time that a majority of voters indicated a preference for full statehood.

ROCKS GLASS

2 OUNCES CHAIRMAN'S AGED RUM

⅜ OUNCE TEMPUS FUGIT CRÈME DE CACAO

1 BARSPOON ALLSPICE DRAM

1 BARSPOON CAMPARI

2 DASHES ANGOSTURA BITTERS

2 DASHES ORANGE BITTERS

Build in a mixing glass. Stir, strain, and pour over a large piece of ice in a double rocks glass.

★ NOTE ★

Allspice dram, also known as pimento dram, is an allspice-flavored liqueur originally made in Jamaica. Wray and Nephew imported a version until the 1980s. St. Elizabeth Allspice Dram has been available since 2008.

PRETTY PRINCESS

A tall tale surrounding the origin of the Manhattan cocktail holds that it was created either by or for Jennie Spencer-Churchill, a New York heiress, to celebrate the election of Samuel Tilden as New York's governor. The only problem with the story is that we know she was in London at the time, about to give birth, later that month, to Winston Churchill. Whatever its true beginning, the Manhattan became an established cocktail by the 1880s, predating other vermouth classics such as the Martinez, martini, Rob Roy, and Bobby Burns. In this variation, rum takes pride of place instead of whiskey as the base spirit.

COUPE

2 OUNCES APPLETON V/X RUM

1 OUNCE ANTICA CARPANO SWEET VERMOUTH

2 DASHES ANGOSTURA BITTERS

BRANDIED CHERRY FOR GARNISH

Stir all ingredients over ice, and strain into a chilled coupe. Garnish with a cherry.

★ NOTE ★

Vermouth is enjoying a worldwide revival in popularity. But red, sweet, or Italian vermouth—however you describe it—isn't made from red wine at all. It's made from a white wine base. The brand we prefer, Antica Carpano, uses a mixture of Piedmont Muscatel and other area white wines, spiced with cinnamon, dates, star anise, and vanilla. (Other sweet vermouths often contain a citrus element, such as orange and/or lemon peel.) As with all fortified wines, always refrigerate after opening.

PUNCHES

Punch existed long before the single-serving cocktail. The first written reference to rum in English appears around 1630. From that point forward, wherever there was rum, there was punch. The word itself derives from the Hindi word *panch*, which means "five" and indicates the five core ingredients: spirit, water, citrus, sweetener, and spice. From the royal family to ruthless pirates, everyone drank punch. Even Père Jean-Baptiste Labat—a French priest, engineer, and sugar developer—had his own punch recipe.

Punches are meant to be shared communally, so each recipe in this chapter gives two versions: The first is larger, for six people, and meant to be built in a pitcher, stirred briefly on ice, poured into a punch bowl with large chunks of ice and fruit garnish, and ladled into punch glasses. The second version is a single serving, meant to be built in a shaking tin and poured into a glass.

Stirring the large-format version only begins to chill the mixture. Adding fresh ice will dilute it further, but the ice for a punch needs to have a large surface area in order to melt slowly. You can find large-format ice cube trays—spheres or cubes—at most kitchen goods stores or, in a pinch, you can make large blocks from clean surplus takeout containers.

LA IMPERATRIZ

Teresa Cristina de Bourbon, a Spanish princess of the kingdom of the Two Sicilies, became empress of Brazil by marrying Emperor Pedro II in 1843. This punch, named for the Brazilian prefecture named for her, honors her Italian heritage with zucca, an aperitif made with rhubarb.

PUNCH BOWL

36 MINT LEAVES, PLUS EXTRA FOR GARNISH

18 LARGE BLACKBERRIES, PLUS EXTRA FOR GARNISH

3 OUNCES HONEY SYRUP (PAGE 11)

6 OUNCES CHAIRMAN'S RESERVE RUM

6 OUNCES RITTENHOUSE RYE

3 OUNCES ZUCCA

4½ OUNCES LEMON JUICE

6 OUNCES DRY SPARKLING WINE

LEMON FOR GARNISH

In a large pitcher, muddle mint and blackberries in honey syrup. Add remaining ingredients, except sparkling wine. Stir with ice cubes for 20 to 30 seconds. Fine strain through mesh strainer into a punch bowl with 3 large ice cubes. Top with sparkling wine, and garnish with mint, blackberries, and lemon wheels.

SINGLE SERVING

FLUTE

6 MINT LEAVES, PLUS EXTRA FOR GARNISH

3 LARGE BLACKBERRIES, PLUS EXTRA FOR GARNISH

½ OUNCE HONEY SYRUP (PAGE 11)

1 OUNCE CHAIRMAN'S RESERVE RUM

1 OUNCE RITTENHOUSE RYE

½ OUNCE ZUCCA

¾ OUNCE LEMON JUICE

1 OUNCE DRY SPARKLING WINE

LEMON FOR GARNISH

Muddle mint and blackberries in honey syrup. Add remaining ingredients except sparkling wine, and shake with ice. Double strain into a flute or Collins glass filled with ice. Top with sparkling wine, and garnish as above.

TWENTY-FIRST AMENDMENT PUNCH

The Eighteenth Amendment, ratified in January 1919 and effective a year later, established Prohibition in the United States. Bacardi, still a Cuban company, tried to pay shareholders in rum before the dissolution of their American holdings, calling it a distribution of "stock." About $50,000 worth found its way to the Holliswood Hall Inn in the hometown of Supervising Enforcement Officer James Shevlin. "Rum Distribution a Clever Scheme," screamed a *Brooklyn Eagle* headline. But the best way to avoid the law was to get out of town. Many American hospitality professionals picked up and headed to Cuba. Ed Donovan from Newark, New Jersey, packed up every piece of his business—chairs, tables, mirrors, hanging sink, and the bar itself—and set it down in Havana. Thankfully, America came to its senses, and the Twenty-First Amendment repealed Prohibition in December 1933. Cheers to that!

PUNCH BOWL

6 OUNCES COGNAC

6 OUNCES SMITH & CROSS RUM

3 OUNCES WHITE WHISKEY

4½ OUNCES SIMPLE SYRUP (PAGE 10)

6 OUNCES LEMON JUICE

12 DASHES ANGOSTURA BITTERS

6 OUNCES DRY SPARKLING WINE

LEMON, ORANGE, AND GRAPES FOR GARNISH

Stir all ingredients except sparkling wine with ice cubes in a large pitcher for 20 to 30 seconds. Strain into a punch bowl with three large ice cubes. Top with sparkling wine, and garnish with lemon wheels, orange slices, and grapes.

COLLINS GLASS

1 OUNCE COGNAC

1 OUNCE SMITH & CROSS RUM

½ OUNCE WHITE WHISKEY

¾ OUNCE SIMPLE SYRUP (PAGE 10)

1 OUNCE LEMON JUICE

2 DASHES ANGOSTURA BITTERS

1 OUNCE DRY SPARKLING WINE

LEMON, ORANGE, AND GRAPES FOR GARNISH

Shake all ingredients except sparkling wine with ice, and double strain into a Collins glass filled with ice. Top and garnish as above.

ALABAZAM

Leo Engel, an American in London, crafted this punch at the bar of the opulent Criterion Hotel near Piccadilly Circus. The hotel restaurant made a famous appearance a decade later in the first Sherlock Holmes story, *A Study in Scarlet*, the title of which matches the color of this drink. The original punch is made with cognac, but we've selected a Jamaican rum that mimics the full body and dark fruit notes of a brandy.

PUNCH BOWL

12 OUNCES APPLETON ESTATE 12 YEAR RUM

9 OUNCES LILLET ROUGE

3 OUNCES LUXARDO MARASCHINO

6 OUNCES SIMPLE SYRUP (PAGE 10)

3 OUNCES LEMON JUICE

12 DASH ANGOSTURA BITTERS

6 OUNCES DRY SPARKLING WINE

LEMONS AND RASPBERRIES FOR GARNISH

Stir all ingredients except sparkling wine with ice cubes in a large pitcher for 20 to 30 seconds. Strain into a punch bowl with 3 large ice cubes. Top with sparkling wine, and garnish with lemon wheels and raspberries.

SINGLE SERVING

FIZZ GLASS

2 OUNCES APPLETON ESTATE 12 YEAR RUM

¾ OUNCES LILLET ROUGE

¼ OUNCE MARASCHINO

½ OUNCE SIMPLE SYRUP (PAGE 10)

¼ OUNCE LEMON JUICE

1 DASH ANGOSTURA BITTERS

1 OUNCE DRY SPARKLING WINE

LEMONS AND RASPBERRIES FOR GARNISH

Shake all ingredients except sparkling wine with ice. Strain into a fizz glass filled with ice. Top with dry sparkling wine, and garnish as above.

PONCHE PIMMS

James Pimm offered a gin-based tonic, containing a secret mixture of herbs and liqueurs, at the London oyster bar that he opened near Buckingham Palace in 1823. That drink became known as Pimm's No. 1. His company went on to produce five other styles with different bases, Pimm's No. 4 using rum. The Distillers Company, which later bought the brand, phased out the less popular variants in 1970, including No. 4. This punch reinterprets the Pimm's No. 4 Cup, a classic summer drink perfect for Caribbean climes.

PUNCH BOWL

18 CUCUMBER SLICES, PLUS EXTRA FOR GARNISH

36 MINT LEAVES, PLUS EXTRA FOR GARNISH

3 OUNCES SIMPLE SYRUP (PAGE 10)

6 OUNCES FLOR DE CAÑA 4 YEAR EXTRA DRY RUM

6 OUNCES PIMM'S NO. 1

3 OUNCES BEEFEATER GIN

1½ OUNCES AMARO CIOCIARO

3 OUNCES GRAPEFRUIT JUICE

3 OUNCES LEMON JUICE

6 OUNCES CLUB SODA

GRAPEFRUIT, LEMON, AND RASPBERRIES FOR GARNISH

Muddle cucumber and mint in syrup. Add remaining ingredients except club soda, and stir with ice cubes in a large pitcher for 20 to 30 seconds. Fine strain through a mesh strainer into a punch bowl with 3 large ice cubes. Top with club soda, and garnish with mint leaves, cucumber slices, grapefruit slices, lemon wheels, and raspberries.

SINGLE SERVING

BEER GLASS

3 CUCUMBER SLICES,
PLUS EXTRA FOR GARNISH

6 MINT LEAVES, PLUS EXTRA FOR GARNISH

½ OUNCE SIMPLE SYRUP (PAGE 10)

1 OUNCE FLOR DE CAÑA
4 YEAR EXTRA DRY RUM

1 OUNCE PIMM'S NO. 1

½ OUNCE BEEFEATER GIN

¼ OUNCE AMARO CIOCIARO

½ OUNCE GRAPEFRUIT JUICE

½ OUNCE LEMON JUICE

1 OUNCE CLUB SODA

GRAPEFRUIT, LEMON, AND
RASPBERRIES FOR GARNISH

Muddle cucumber and mint in syrup. Add remaining ingredients except club soda, shake with ice, and double strain into beer glass. Top and garnish as above.

A View of the City of the Havana, taken from the Road near Colonel Howe's Battery.
Vue de La ville de La Havane prise du chemin près de La batterie du Colonel Howe. | Vista de la Ciudad de la Havana desde el camino de la batería del Coronel Howe.
Drawn by Elias Durnford Engineer, Etchd by Paul Sandby, & Engraved by Edw.d Rooker.
London Publish'd according to Act of Parliament Feb.y 15th 1764 by Tho.s Jefferys the Corner of S.t Martins Lane.

ERNESTO

This punch interprets the Hemingway Daiquirí (page 118) and adds Fernet Branca, an Italian amaro that provides a bitter, herbal undertone. Making cocktails with Fernet Branca often proves difficult because of its powerful nature, much like this punch's writerly namesake.

PUNCH BOWL

12 OUNCES EL DORADO 3 YEAR RUM

2¼ OUNCES FERNET BRANCA

1½ OUNCES MARASCHINO

4½ OUNCES SIMPLE SYRUP (PAGE 10)

4½ OUNCES LIME JUICE

3 OUNCES GRAPEFRUIT JUICE

6 OUNCES RED WINE

ORANGE, LIME, AND GRAPES FOR GARNISH

Stir all ingredients except wine with ice cubes in a large pitcher for 20 to 30 seconds. Strain into a punch bowl with 3 large ice cubes. Top with wine, and garnish with orange slices, lime wheels, and grapes.

SINGLE SERVING

PUNCH GLASS

2 OUNCES EL DORADO 3 YEAR RUM

⅜ OUNCE FERNET BRANCA

¼ OUNCE MARASCHINO

¾ OUNCE SIMPLE SYRUP (PAGE 10)

¾ OUNCE LIME JUICE

½ OUNCE GRAPEFRUIT JUICE

1 OUNCE RED WINE

ORANGE, LIME, AND GRAPES FOR GARNISH

Shake all ingredients except red wine with ice, and strain into a punch glass. Float red wine on top using the underside of a teaspoon held just above the drink's surface. Garnish as above.

HOTEL NACIONAL

The Hotel Nacional opened in Havana in December 1930 and since then has hosted a bevy of illustrious guests—and a mob summit. At least three great barmen called it home: Eddie Woelke, Fred Kaufman, and Wil Taylor. Cocktail author Charles Baker attributes the Hotel Nacional Special cocktail to Taylor, who, like many others, had managed the bar at the Waldorf-Astoria before Prohibition brought him to Cuba. In 1933, as a battle between Batista and his ousted predecessor, Julio Sanguil y Echarte, raged around the hotel, Taylor continued mixing drinks, which Baker continued to imbibe.

PUNCH BOWL

12 OUNCES APPLETON ESTATE 12 YEAR RUM

1½ OUNCES APRICOT BRANDY

3 OUNCES SIMPLE SYRUP (PAGE 10)

6 OUNCES PINEAPPLE JUICE

3 OUNCES LIME JUICE

6 OUNCES DRY SPARKLING WINE

LIME AND MINT LEAVES FOR GARNISH

Stir all ingredients except sparkling wine with ice cubes in a large pitcher for 20 to 30 seconds. Strain into a punch bowl with 3 large ice cubes. Top with sparkling wine, and garnish with lime wheels and mint leaves.

SINGLE SERVING

COLLINS GLASS

2 OUNCES APPLETON ESTATE 12 YEAR RUM

¼ OUNCE APRICOT BRANDY

½ OUNCE SIMPLE SYRUP (PAGE 10)

1 OUNCE PINEAPPLE JUICE

½ OUNCE LIME JUICE

1 OUNCE DRY SPARKLING WINE

LIME AND MINT LEAVES FOR GARNISH

Shake all ingredients except sparkling wine with ice, and strain into a Collins glass filled with ice. Top and garnish as above.

HAVANA HARBOR SPECIAL

While safeguarding American concerns at the end of the Cuban War of Independence, the USS *Maine* exploded in Havana Harbor on February 15, 1898. As a result the United States declared war on Spain to chants of "Remember the Maine, to Hell with Spain!" The Remember the Maine cocktail first appeared in Charles Baker's 1939 *Gentleman's Companion*. The original doesn't include lemon juice or simple syrup, added here for freshness.

PUNCH BOWL

12 OUNCES CHAIRMAN'S RESERVE RUM

6 OUNCES SWEET VERMOUTH

3 OUNCES CHERRY HEERING

3 OUNCES SIMPLE SYRUP (PAGE 10)

4½ OUNCES LEMON JUICE

12 DASHES ABSINTHE

12 DASHES ANGOSTURA BITTERS

6 OUNCES CLUB SODA

LEMON, ORANGE, AND GRAPES FOR GARNISH

Stir all ingredients except club soda with ice cubes in a large pitcher for 20 to 30 seconds. Strain into a punch bowl with 3 large ice cubes. Top with club soda, and garnish with lemon wheels, orange slices, and grapes.

SINGLE SERVING

COLLINS GLASS

2 OUNCES CHAIRMAN'S RESERVE RUM

1 OUNCE SWEET VERMOUTH

½ OUNCE CHERRY HEERING

½ OUNCE SIMPLE SYRUP (PAGE 10)

¾ OUNCE LEMON JUICE

2 DASHES ABSINTHE

2 DASHES ANGOSTURA BITTERS

1 OUNCE CLUB SODA

LEMON, ORANGE, AND GRAPES FOR GARNISH

Shake all ingredients except club soda with ice, and strain into a Collins glass filled with ice. Top and garnish as above.

LAFAYETTE

Created in the midst of an Indian summer, this drink takes its name from a town near Syracuse, New York, known for its apple orchards. Drink it on the last day of summer.

PUNCH BOWL

6 OUNCES BEEFEATER GIN

6 OUNCES FLOR DE CAÑA 4 YEAR EXTRA DRY RUM

4½ OUNCES GINGER SYRUP (PAGE 10)

6 OUNCES GREEN APPLE JUICE

4½ OUNCES LEMON JUICE

12 DASHES PEYCHAUD'S BITTERS

6 OUNCES CLUB SODA

APPLE AND LEMON FOR GARNISH

Stir with ice cubes in a large pitcher for 20 to 30 seconds. Strain into a punch bowl with 3 large ice cubes. Top with club soda, and garnish with apple slices and lemon wheels.

SINGLE SERVING

BEER GLASS

1 OUNCE BEEFEATER GIN

1 OUNCE FLOR DE CAÑA 4 YEAR
  EXTRA DRY RUM

¾ OUNCE GINGER SYRUP (PAGE 10)

1 OUNCE GREEN APPLE JUICE

¾ OUNCE LEMON JUICE

2 DASHES PEYCHAUD'S BITTERS

1 OUNCE CLUB SODA

APPLE AND LEMON FOR GARNISH

Shake with ice, and strain into a beer glass. Top and garnish as above.

RUBY STAR PUNCH

The grapefruit bitters in this punch—named for a rare type of ruby similar in color—pull citrus notes from and enhance the rhubarb notes of the zucca amaro, while the aged rum balances the rest of the drink.

PUNCH BOWL

12 OUNCES MOUNT GAY ECLIPSE RUM

3 OUNCES ZUCCA

4½ OUNCES RHUBARB SYRUP (PAGE 11)

4½ OUNCES LIME JUICE

4½ OUNCES ORANGE JUICE

1 OUNCE RHUM CLÉMENT CRÉOLE SHRUBB

12 DASHES GRAPEFRUIT BITTERS

ORANGE AND LIME FOR GARNISH

Stir with ice cubes in a large pitcher for 20 to 30 seconds. Strain into a punch bowl with 3 large ice cubes. Garnish with orange slices and lime wheels.

Rhum Clément Créole Shrubb is a liqueur made from white and aged rums and flavored with Caribbean spices and orange peel. If you can't find Créole Shrubb, substitute with orange curaçao.

SINGLE SERVING

ROCKS GLASS

2 OUNCES MOUNT GAY ECLIPSE RUM

½ OUNCE ZUCCA

¾ OUNCE RHUBARB SYRUP (PAGE 11)

¾ OUNCE LIME JUICE

¾ OUNCE ORANGE JUICE

1 TEASPOON RHUM CLÉMENT CRÉOLE SHRUBB

2 DASHES GRAPEFRUIT BITTERS

ORANGE AND LIME FOR GARNISH

Shake with ice, and strain into a rocks glass with ice. Garnish as above.

HONEY BADGER

The honey badger is a feisty animal, and so is this drink. The jalapeños in the hot honey syrup give it kick, but you can always adjust the heat level to taste. The honey badger don't care.

PUNCH BOWL

9 OUNCES FLOR DE CAÑA 4 YEAR RUM

6 OUNCES LAIRD'S APPLEJACK

3 OUNCES HOT HONEY SYRUP (PAGE 11)

3 OUNCES PASSION FRUIT SYRUP (PAGE 11)

4½ OUNCES LIME JUICE

APPLE AND JALAPEÑO FOR GARNISH

Stir with ice cubes in a large pitcher for 20 to 30 seconds. Strain into a punch bowl with 3 large ice cubes. Garnish with apple slices and jalapeño wheels.

SINGLE SERVING

PUNCH GLASS

1½ OUNCES FLOR DE CAÑA 4 YEAR RUM

1 OUNCE LAIRD'S APPLEJACK

½ OUNCE HOT HONEY SYRUP (PAGE 11)

½ OUNCE PASSION FRUIT SYRUP (PAGE 11)

¾ OUNCE LIME JUICE

APPLE AND JALAPEÑO FOR GARNISH

Shake with ice, and strain into a punch glass. Garnish as above.

FUNKY OLD MAN FROM MARTINIQUE

This punch recipe pays homage to the Old Cuban by Audrey Saunders (page 99) and excellently showcases the unique flavors of agricole rhum: The sweet grassiness shines, gently enhanced by the other ingredients.

PUNCH BOWL

12 OUNCES LA FAVORITE AMBRE OR VIEUX RHUM

4½ OUNCES CANE SYRUP

6 OUNCES LIME JUICE

18 DASHES ANGOSTURA BITTERS

6 OUNCES DRY SPARKLING WINE

LIME AND MINT LEAVES FOR GARNISH

Stir all ingredients except sparkling wine with ice cubes in a large pitcher for 20 to 30 seconds, and strain into a punch bowl with 3 large ice cubes. Top with sparkling wine, and garnish with lime wheels and mint leaves.

SINGLE SERVING

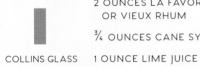

COLLINS GLASS

2 OUNCES LA FAVORITE AMBRE OR VIEUX RHUM

¾ OUNCES CANE SYRUP

1 OUNCE LIME JUICE

3 DASHES ANGOSTURA BITTERS

1 OUNCE DRY SPARKLING WINE

LIME AND MINT LEAVES FOR GARNISH

Shake all ingredients except sparkling wine with ice, and strain into a Collins glass filled with ice. Top and garnish as above.

ANCHOR PUNCH

Muhammad Ali used the anchor punch to knock out Sonny Liston in the first round of their 1965 rematch. Now you can drink like the champ.

PUNCH BOWL

12 OUNCES SAILOR JERRY RUM

4½ OUNCES APRICOT BRANDY

4½ OUNCES GINGER SYRUP (PAGE 10)

4½ OUNCES GUAVA PUREE

4½ OUNCES LIME JUICE

LIME, ORANGE, AND FRESH NUTMEG FOR GARNISH

Stir with ice cubes in a large pitcher for 20 to 30 seconds. Strain into a punch bowl with 3 large ice cubes. Garnish with lime wheels, orange slices, and freshly grated nutmeg.

SINGLE SERVING

PUNCH GLASS

2 OUNCES SAILOR JERRY RUM

¾ OUNCES APRICOT BRANDY

¾ OUNCES GINGER SYRUP (PAGE 10)

¾ OUNCES GUAVA PUREE

¾ OUNCES LIME JUICE

LIME, ORANGE, AND FRESH NUTMEG FOR GARNISH

Shake with ice, and strain into a punch glass. Garnish as above.

GUN CLUB PUNCH

Ernest Hemingway isn't the only author who enjoyed hunting from time to time. This classic comes from *Trader Vic's Bartender's Guide* (1972) and is meant to be served in a decorative green mug in the shape of a shotgun shell.

PUNCH BOWL

6 OUNCES HAMILTON JAMAICAN RUM

6 OUNCES WHITE CUBAN RUM OR EL DORADO 3 YEAR RUM

3 OUNCES DRY CURAÇAO

2¼ OUNCES POMEGRANATE MOLASSES

1½ OUNCES SIMPLE SYRUP (PAGE 10)

6 OUNCES PINEAPPLE JUICE

4½ OUNCES LIME JUICE

PINEAPPLE FOR GARNISH

Stir with ice cubes in a large pitcher for 20 to 30 seconds. Strain into a punch bowl with 3 large ice cubes. Garnish with pineapple slices.

The original recipe called for grenadine instead of pomegranate syrup, but the latter, which you can find at larger grocery stores, has a more intense pomegranate flavor that benefits the drink.

SINGLE SERVING

PUNCH GLASS

1 OUNCE HAMILTON JAMAICAN RUM

1 OUNCE WHITE CUBAN RUM OR EL DORADO 3 YEAR RUM

½ OUNCE DRY CURAÇAO

⅜ OUNCE POMEGRANATE MOLASSES

¼ OUNCE SIMPLE SYRUP (PAGE 10)

1 OUNCE PINEAPPLE JUICE

¾ OUNCE LIME JUICE

PINEAPPLE FOR GARNISH

Shake with ice, and strain into a punch glass. Garnish as above.

GREEN SLIPPER PUNCH

When the first buds of greenery start to show after a long, hard winter, it's time for a Green Slipper. The apple, mint, and cucumber provide a ménage of freshness, which the sweetness of the St. Germain enhances with floral notes. This cocktail brims with springtime hopes.

PUNCH BOWL

36 MINT LEAVES, PLUS EXTRA FOR GARNISH

18 APPLE SLICES, PLUS EXTRA FOR GARNISH

18 CUCUMBER SLICES, PLUS EXTRA FOR GARNISH

6 OUNCES FLOR DE CAÑA 4 YEAR EXTRA DRY RUM

3 OUNCES ST. GERMAIN

4½ OUNCES SIMPLE SYRUP (PAGE 10)

6 OUNCES LIME JUICE

CUCUMBER, GREEN APPLE, AND MINT LEAVES FOR GARNISH

Blend all ingredients in a countertop blender for 20 to 30 seconds. Fine strain through a mesh strainer into a punch bowl with 3 large ice cubes. Garnish with cucumber slices, green apple slices, and mint.

SINGLE SERVING

COLLINS GLASS

6 MINT LEAVES, PLUS EXTRA FOR GARNISH

3 GREEN APPLE SLICES, PLUS EXTRA FOR GARNISH

3 CUCUMBER SLICES, PLUS EXTRA FOR GARNISH

¾ OUNCE SIMPLE SYRUP (PAGE 10)

2 OUNCES FLOR DE CAÑA 4 YEAR EXTRA DRY RUM

½ OUNCE ST. GERMAIN

1 OUNCE LIME JUICE

Blend all ingredients, and double strain into a punch glass or small Collins glass filled with ice. Garnish with additional apple slices and mint.

PONCHE POR AVION

Hot honey and agricole rhum spice up this Caribbean take on the Airmail cocktail (page 86). Barbancourt Blanc is very aromatic with strong vanilla notes that easily complement and round out the spicy honey.

PUNCH BOWL

12 OUNCES BARBANCOURT BLANC RUM

4½ OUNCES HOT HONEY SYRUP (PAGE 11)

4½ OUNCES LIME JUICE

6 OUNCES DRY SPARKLING WINE

LIME, JALAPEÑO, AND MINT LEAVES FOR GARNISH

Stir all ingredients except sparkling wine with ice cubes in a large pitcher for 20 to 30 seconds. Strain into a punch bowl with 3 large ice cubes. Top with sparkling wine, and garnish with lime wheels, jalapeños wheels, and mint leaves.

SINGLE SERVING

FLUTE

2 OUNCES BARBANCOURT BLANC

¾ OUNCES HOT HONEY SYRUP (PAGE 11)

¾ OUNCES LIME JUICE

1 OUNCE DRY SPARKLING WINE

LIME, JALAPEÑO, AND MINT LEAVES FOR GARNISH

Shake all ingredients except sparkling wine with ice, and strain into a flute. Top and garnish as above.

PEACH JAM PUNCH

Preserves have long been used to capture and maintain seasonal flavors for later enjoyment. With this botanical-forward recipe, summer's just a sip away. The J. M. Blanc, a light agricole rhum, pairs nicely with the rose and cucumber notes of Hendrick's gin.

PUNCH BOWL

6 OUNCES J. M. BLANC RHUM

4½ OUNCES HENDRICK'S GIN

3 OUNCES PEACH BRANDY

3 OUNCES LEMON JUICE

6 TEASPOONS PEACH JAM

6 OUNCES DRY SPARKLING WINE

CUCUMBER FOR GARNISH

Stir all ingredients except sparkling wine with ice cubes in a large pitcher for 20 to 30 seconds. Strain into a punch bowl with 3 large ice cubes. Top with sparkling wine, and garnish with cucumber slices.

SINGLE SERVING

COLLINS GLASS

1 OUNCE J. M. BLANC RHUM

¾ OUNCE HENDRICK'S GIN

½ OUNCE PEACH BRANDY

½ OUNCE LEMON JUICE

1 TEASPOON PEACH JAM

1 OUNCE DRY SPARKLING WINE

CUCUMBER FOR GARNISH

Shake all ingredients except sparkling wine with ice, and strain into a Collins glass filled with ice. Top and garnish as above.

CARIBBEAN FISH HOUSE PUNCH

Fish House Punch dates back to 1732 in Philadelphia, where members of the first angling club in the British North American colonies partook of a bowl or two. George Washington, born that same year, later enjoyed it as well. After one encounter with the punch, it's said that he couldn't make an entry in his diary for the next three days.

PUNCH BOWL

6 OUNCES COGNAC

4½ OUNCES SMITH & CROSS RUM

3 OUNCES PEACH BRANDY

1½ OUNCE MARASCHINO

3 OUNCES SIMPLE SYRUP (PAGE 10)

4½ OUNCES LEMON JUICE

LEMON AND GRAPES FOR GARNISH

Stir with ice cubes in a large pitcher for 20 to 30 seconds. Strain into a punch bowl with 3 large ice cubes. Garnish with lemon wheels and grapes.

SINGLE SERVING

PUNCH GLASS

1 OUNCE COGNAC

¾ OUNCE SMITH & CROSS RUM

½ OUNCE PEACH BRANDY

¼ OUNCE MARASCHINO

½ OUNCE SIMPLE SYRUP (PAGE 10)

¾ OUNCE LEMON JUICE

LEMON AND GRAPES FOR
  GARNISH

Shake with ice, and strain into a punch glass. Garnish as above.

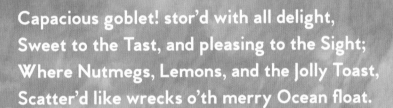

Capacious goblet! stor'd with all delight,
Sweet to the Tast, and pleasing to the Sight;
Where Nutmegs, Lemons, and the Jolly Toast,
Scatter'd like wrecks o'th merry Ocean float.

—ANNE FINCH, FROM "VERSES ON A PUNCH-BOWL" (1701)

MASALA MANGO PANCH

In addition to West African slaves, the British, Dutch, and French transported Indian laborers to the Caribbean, and Cuba has a population of more than 30,000 Indo-Caribbeans, as their descendants are known today. The inspiration for this drink came from a snack of mangoes covered with chili and salt spotted along the boardwalk of Brighton Beach in New York City, and the recipe returns the word "punch" to its flavorful roots.

PUNCH BOWL

6 OUNCES FLOR DE CAÑA 7 YEAR RUM

4½ OUNCES APPLETON ESTATE V/X RUM

6 OUNCES MANGO PUREE

4½ OUNCES CHILI SYRUP (PAGE 10)

3 OUNCES LIME JUICE

¾ TEASPOON CURRY POWDER

LIME FOR GARNISH

Stir with ice cubes in a large pitcher for 20 to 30 seconds. Strain into a punch bowl with 3 large ice cubes. Garnish with lime wheels.

SINGLE SERVING

PUNCH GLASS

1 OUNCE FLOR DE CAÑA 7 YEAR RUM

¾ OUNCE APPLETON ESTATE V/X RUM

1 OUNCE MANGO PUREE

¾ OUNCE CHILI SYRUP (PAGE 10)

½ OUNCE LIME JUICE

1 PINCH CURRY POWDER

LIME FOR GARNISH

Shake with ice, and strain into a punch glass. Garnish as above.

You know from Eastern India came

The skill of making punch as did the name.

And as the name consists of letters five,

By five ingredients is it kept alive.

To purest water sugar must be joined,

With these the grateful acid is combined.

Some any sours they get contented use,

But men of taste do that from Tagus choose.

When now these three are mixed with care

Then added be of spirit a small share.

And that you may the drink quite perfect see,

Atop the musky nut must grated be.

—SAMUEL MATHER
IN A NOTE TO CHARLES FRANKLAND (1757)

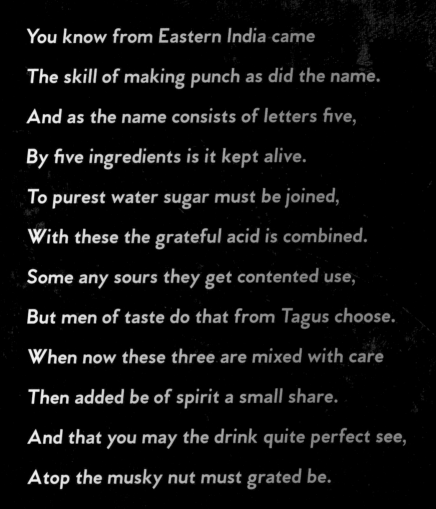

VESPERONE PUNCH

The end-of-summer blackberries and autumnal sage restrain the heavy-hitting rum, rye, and chartreuse in this drink.

PUNCH BOWL

24 BLACKBERRIES, PLUS EXTRA FOR GARNISH

12 SAGE LEAVES, PLUS EXTRA FOR GARNISH

3 OUNCES AGAVE SYRUP (PAGE 10)

6 OUNCES RON ZACAPA

6 OUNCES RYE

3 OUNCES GREEN CHARTREUSE

3 OUNCES LIME JUICE

6 OUNCES DRY SPARKLING WINE

LIME FOR GARNISH

Muddle sage and blackberries in the syrup. Add remaining ingredients except sparkling wine, and stir with ice cubes in a large pitcher for 20 to 30 seconds. Fine strain through a mesh strainer into a punch bowl with 3 large ice cubes. Top with sparkling wine, and garnish with lime and additional sage leaves and blackberries.

SINGLE SERVING

COLLINS GLASS

4 BLACKBERRIES, PLUS EXTRA FOR GARNISH

2 SAGE LEAVES, PLUS EXTRA FOR GARNISH

½ OUNCE AGAVE SYRUP (PAGE 10)

1 OUNCE RON ZACAPA

1 OUNCE RYE WHISKEY

½ OUNCE GREEN CHARTREUSE

½ OUNCE LIME JUICE

1 OUNCE DRY SPARKLING WINE

LIME FOR GARNISH

Muddle sage and blackberries in syrup. Add remaining ingredients except sparkling wine, and shake with ice. Double strain into a Collins glass filled with ice. Top and garnish as above.

OLD NAVY PUNCH

English sailors started receiving rum rations in 1655. Clean drinking water was either hard to find or hard to maintain. Beer lost its flavor and went flat. French brandy and Spanish wine worked but were expensive or hard to obtain. Rum, however, was plentiful. In 1769, the Society of West India Merchants organized and published a booklet about the health benefits of drinking rum. Within a decade, the Naval Provisioning Office was replacing brandy with rum in ship stores, and the Royal Navy didn't abolish rum rations completely until July 31, 1970, known as Black Tot Day. Altered and modified over the centuries, the recipe for Navy Punch exists in countless variations. This is the version we prefer.

PUNCH BOWL

4½ OUNCES COGNAC

3 OUNCES HAMILTON 151 RUM

3 OUNCES PEACH BRANDY

3 OUNCES SIMPLE SYRUP (PAGE 10)

4½ OUNCES LEMON JUICE

3 OUNCES ORANGE JUICE

6 OUNCES DRY SPARKLING WINE

LEMON AND ORANGE FOR GARNISH

Stir all ingredients except sparkling wine with ice cubes in a large pitcher for 20 to 30 seconds. Strain into a punch bowl with 3 large ice cubes. Top with sparkling wine, and garnish with lemon wheels and orange slices.

SINGLE SERVING

COLLINS GLASS

¾ OUNCE COGNAC

½ OUNCE HAMILTON 151 RUM

½ OUNCE PEACH BRANDY

½ OUNCE SIMPLE SYRUP (PAGE 10)

¾ OUNCE LEMON JUICE

½ OUNCE ORANGE JUICE

1 OUNCE DRY SPARKLING WINE

LEMON AND ORANGE
FOR GARNISH

Shake all ingredients except sparkling wine with ice, and strain into a Collins glass filled with ice. Top and garnish as above.

There's nought, no doubt, so much the spirit calms

    As rum and true religion: thus it was,

Some plunder'd, some drank spirits, some sung psalms,

    The high wind made the treble, and as bas

The hoarse harsh waves kept time; fright cured the qualms

    Of all the luckless landsmen's sea-sick maws:

Strange sounds of wailing, blasphemy, devotion,

    Clamour'd in chorus to the roaring ocean.

—LORD BYRON, *DON JUAN* (1819)

PIRATES & THE PUNCH BOWL

Just as punch was all the rage for the English aristocracy, so was it the drink of choice for upwardly mobile pirates. The bandits of the sea often chose their commanders under the influence of punch. One such commander was Welshman John Roberts—but Roberts himself rarely drank and found himself an unwilling participant in piracy when the ship he was on was captured and its new overlord recognized Roberts's navigational skills. The punch bowl may have helped Roberts rise to commander, but his first course of action was to ban drinking below decks at night. His crew understandably chafed at the move. Why take orders from a man who didn't even drink? Roberts had a hard time retaining authority over his crew. He needed a rum-soaked alter ego to control them. Thus he became Bartholomew Roberts, a finely dressed man who shot dead anyone who dared insult him. He came to power by the punch bowl, and by the punch bowl he fell. In February 1722, the HMS *Swallow*, encountering Roberts's fleet of three off Cape Lopez in Gabon, chased and eventually captured one of the ships. Returning to port, the captain of the *Swallow* spotted Roberts's ship, the *Royal Fortune*. The pirates had captured another ship in the meantime and were deep in their cups in celebration. They didn't stand a chance. Roberts was killed by grapeshot while standing on deck, marking an end to the golden age of piracy.

'TI PUNCH

Traveling the Caribbean on assignment for *Harper's* magazine, reporter Lafcadio Hearn discovered 'Ti Punch on Martinique in 1887. It's important to use agricole rhum to provide character and to help differentiate this punch from a Planter's Punch (page 80). This drink has always been served single-style, so no communal recipe. If you do want to serve it to a group, make it in individual glasses. But drink this cocktail in one shot in the morning. Seriously, that's the tradition.

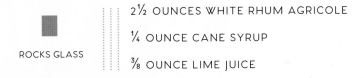

ROCKS GLASS

2½ OUNCES WHITE RHUM AGRICOLE

¼ OUNCE CANE SYRUP

⅜ OUNCE LIME JUICE

Combine all ingredients, including the lime shell(s), over cracked ice in a double rocks glass, and stir.

★ NOTE ★

To make a 'Ti Punch properly, cut the end of a lime into a disk (or butt, as we say), and squeeze the juice into the drink. Adding the shell/butt imparts oils from the rind into the flavor profile. Then bottoms up!

REGENT'S PUNCH

Medical historians have surmised that King George III of Britain suffered from porphyria, which plunged him into his infamous madness. In his stead, his eldest son, Prince George Augustus, served as regent, although the prime minister did most of the actual governing. That left the prince regent with plenty of time to indulge his favorite pastimes: women and punch. A Mr. Madison, his maître d', created this recipe, although the exact proportions are unclear because so many different people made it so many different times to satisfy the prince's enormous thirst.

PUNCH BOWL

3 OUNCES BATAVIA ARRACK

3 OUNCES COGNAC

3 OUNCES CURAÇAO

3 OUNCES SMITH & CROSS RUM

4½ OUNCES SIMPLE SYRUP (PAGE 10)

3 OUNCES GREEN TEA CACHAÇA (PAGE 10)

4½ OUNCES LEMON JUICE

1½ OUNCES PINEAPPLE JUICE

6 DASHES ANGOSTURA BITTERS

6 OUNCES DRY SPARKLING WINE

ORANGE AND LEMON FOR GARNISH

Stir all ingredients except sparkling wine with ice cubes in a large pitcher for 20 to 30 seconds. Strain into a punch bowl with 3 large ice cubes. Top with sparkling wine, and garnish with orange slices and lemon wheels.

For this recipe, we recommend that you use Mãe de Ouro for the green tea–infused cachaça.

SINGLE SERVING

COLLINS GLASS

½ OUNCE BATAVIA ARRACK

½ OUNCE COGNAC

½ OUNCE CURAÇAO

½ OUNCE SMITH & CROSS RUM

¾ OUNCE SIMPLE SYRUP (PAGE 10)

½ OUNCE GREEN TEA CACHAÇA (PAGE 10)

¾ OUNCE LEMON JUICE

¼ OUNCE PINEAPPLE JUICE

1 DASH ANGOSTURA BITTERS

1 OUNCE DRY SPARKLING WINE

ORANGE AND LEMON FOR GARNISH

Shake all ingredients except sparkling wine with ice, and strain into a Collins glass filled with ice. Top and garnish as above.

PLANTER'S PUNCH

In 1845 West Indian planters drank a version made with guava jelly, Madeira, green tea, and cognac. In 1900, a Baltimore journalist tried the Planter's Punch in Jamaica—just one hundred miles south of Cuba—and later called it "a drink that I have esteemed highly ever since." This drink is usually served single-style, so the communal recipe comes second.

SWIZZLE GLASS

2 OUNCES APPLETON 12 YEAR RUM

¾ OUNCE SIMPLE SYRUP (PAGE 10)

1 OUNCE LIME JUICE

1 DASH CURAÇAO

1 DASH ANGOSTURA BITTERS, PLUS EXTRA TO SERVE

1 DASH GRENADINE (PAGE 10)

1 OUNCE CLUB SODA

ORANGE AND CHERRY FOR GARNISH

Whip shake all ingredients except club soda with crushed ice. Strain into a swizzle or Collins glass filled with ice cubes. Top with club soda and bitters to taste, and garnish with an orange slice and brandied or fresh cherry.

COMMUNAL SERVING

PUNCH BOWL

12 OUNCES APPLETON 12 YEAR RUM

4½ OUNCES SIMPLE SYRUP (PAGE 10)

6 OUNCES LIME JUICE

1 OUNCE CURAÇAO

6 DASHES ANGOSTURA BITTERS, PLUS EXTRA TO SERVE

1 OUNCE GRENADINE (PAGE 10)

6 OUNCES CLUB SODA

LIME, ORANGE, AND CHERRIES FOR GARNISH

Stir all ingredients except club soda with ice cubes in a large pitcher for 20 to 30 seconds. Strain into a punch bowl with 3 large ice cubes. Top as above, and garnish with lime wheels, orange slices, and brandied or fresh cherries.

FLIPS & FIZZES

All flips contain egg, which provides distinctive body to a cocktail. (See the description of a loggerhead flip on page 101.) *How to Mix Drinks* by Jerry Thomas was the first bar book to include a flip, and Thomas notes that the "essential in flips of all sorts is to produce the smoothness by repeated pouring back and forward between two vessels and beating up the eggs well." All fizzes contain carbonation of some kind for effervescence. Some fizzes contain egg but not all of them. The addition of egg white makes a silver fizz. The addition of an egg yolk makes a golden fizz. The addition of a whole egg results in a royal fizz. If you use sparkling wine instead of carbonated water, you get a diamond fizz. Got it? Good.

PLATANO DOMINICANO

What grows together goes together. This cocktail exemplifies that culinary decree by pairing rum, coffee, and banana. (The hint of coffee in the cocktail gives it that extra caffeinated kick.) Our inspiration came from Sasha Petraske of Milk & Honey in New York City, who created the Dominicana cocktail, itself a Caribbean variant of the White Russian.

COUPE

2 OUNCES HEAVY CREAM, PLUS EXTRA TO TOP

2 OUNCES BRUGAL EXTRA VIEJO RUM

¾ OUNCE GALLIANO RISTRETTO LIQUEUR

¼ OUNCE GIFFARD BANANE DU BRÉSIL

Dry shake the cream to whip. Stir remaining ingredients over ice, and strain into a chilled coupe. Top with the whipped cream.

★ NOTE ★

Ristretto, which means "restricted" in Italian, describes a short shot of espresso, and the Italians put their espresso knowledge to good use in one of the ingredients in this cocktail. Galliano Ristretto is an espresso liqueur—not to be confused with coffee liqueur. Blending two beans, Robusta and Arabica, it tastes bitter, strong, creamy, and sweet all at the same time.

AIRMAIL

The first instance of the Airmail cocktail appeared in *Esquire* magazine's 1949 edition of *Handbook for Hosts*. This version is a rummier French "75"—think of it as a Cuban 98 that pays homage to that first Pan American flight in October 1927 carrying mail from Key West to Havana (page 36). The honey syrup plays nicely with the notes of banana and orange blossom in the Appleton V/X.

FLUTE

1 OUNCE APPLETON ESTATE V/X RUM

½ OUNCE HONEY SYRUP (PAGE 11)

½ OUNCE LIME JUICE

3 OUNCES DRY SPARKLING WINE

LIME FOR GARNISH

Shake rum, syrup, and lime juice with ice, and strain into a flute. Top with sparkling wine, and garnish with lime.

★ **NOTE** ★

Honey might seem like a relatively simple ingredient, but in America alone there are around 300 different varieties. Clover honey predominates, but do a little legwork and you'll discover many other options. In California, Florida, and Texas, you'll often find orange blossom honey, which uses a combination of several different citruses, primarily orange flower. Blueberry honey appears throughout New England and Michigan, and eucalyptus honey, if you can find it, has a slightly astringent aftertaste. Using one of these different types of honey will change the flavor profile of your cocktail. It's a great way to put your own stamp on a drink.

GOLDEN RAISIN FIZZ

The inspiration for this cocktail came from rum raisin ice cream on a tropical summer day. This golden fizz pulls vanilla notes from the Galliano, and the raisin-infused rum imparts the tangy richness of the dried fruit. The historical pairing of rum and raisins begins not in Cuba or even Spain but in Sicily and with a different alcohol altogether. Málaga gelato—named for the Spanish source of the grapes—originally was made with wine-soaked raisins. Rum raisin ice cream first gained popularity in America in the 1930s, reaching its peak in the 1980s with the Häagen-Dazs version.

FIZZ GLASS

2 OUNCES RAISIN-INFUSED RUM (PAGE 11)

¼ OUNCE GALLIANO

½ OUNCE SIMPLE SYRUP (PAGE 10)

1 TEASPOON SWEETENED CONDENSED MILK

1 EGG YOLK

1 OUNCE CLUB SODA

RUM-SOAKED RAISINS FOR GARNISH

Dry shake all ingredients except club soda, then shake again with ice. Strain into a fizz glass with ice. Top with club soda, and garnish with rum-soaked raisins.

★ NOTE ★

For this recipe, we recommend that you use Mount Gay Eclipse for the raisin-infused rum.

IMPERIAL FIZZ

Rum and rye are the only two R's you need. Despite their convenient alliteration—or perhaps because of it—rum and rye really are a classic spirit pairing. This drink appeared in Hugo Ensslin's 1916 *Recipes for Mixed Drinks*. The spicy Rittenhouse Rye balances the banana- and orange-forward Appleton V/X. Both spirits convey a lot of heat that the egg white tempers on the palate.

COLLINS GLASS

1 OUNCE APPLETON V/X RUM

1 OUNCE RITTENHOUSE RYE

¾ OUNCE SIMPLE SYRUP (PAGE 10)

¾ OUNCE LEMON JUICE

1 EGG WHITE

ORANGE FOR GARNISH

Dry shake all ingredients, then shake again with ice. Pour into a fizz glass or small Collins glass, and garnish with an orange twist.

"A Fizz, you see, was what a sporting man would moisten the clay with directly upon arising—an eye-opener, corpse-reviver, fog-cutter, gloom-lifter, what-have-you. A hangover cure. Into the saloon you'd go, the kindly internist behind the bar would manipulate a bottle or two, and zam!"

—DAVID WONDRICH

ISLE OF MANHATTAN FIZZ

In 2010, Amanda Hesser, food editor of the *New York Times Magazine* and author of the best-selling *Essential New York Times Cookbook* (and now a James Beard and IACP Award winner), wrote a Recipe Redux column about New York City mayor Ed Koch's favorite cocktail. In 1987 he had chosen the Coconut Daiquirí, which narrowly beat out the Ramos Gin Fizz, both as made by his friend David Margolis. Hesser asked us to come up with a new version of the daiquirí, so we created this hybrid of hizzoner's two favorites in fizz form. The coconut puree mimics the texture of the egg and cream of a Ramos Gin Fizz, while the pineapple juice and rum recall the piña colada (masquerading as a daiquirí).

COLLINS GLASS

¾ OUNCE GIN

¾ OUNCE WHITE RUM

2 OUNCES COCONUT PUREE

¾ OUNCE SIMPLE SYRUP (PAGE 10)

½ OUNCE LIME JUICE

½ OUNCE PINEAPPLE JUICE

4 DROPS ORANGE FLOWER WATER

1½ OUNCES CLUB SODA

LIME FOR GARNISH

Combine all ingredients except club soda, and dry shake. Shake again with ice, and strain into a Collins glass with cubed ice. Top with club soda, and garnish with lime zest.

CHICAGO FIZZ

During Prohibition—which Will Rogers famously described as "better than no liquor at all"—former saloon keepers and bartenders from Chicago supposedly were arriving in Cuba at the rate of twelve per day. The precise origins of this drink are unknown. We know it was served at the Waldorf-Astoria Hotel in New York City before Prohibition—but that's about all we know about its genesis. Despite its obscure origins, this is a smooth classic that has stuck around.

COLLINS GLASS

1 OUNCE PORT

1 OUNCE RON ZACAPA RUM

½ OUNCE SIMPLE SYRUP (PAGE 10)

½ OUNCE LEMON JUICE

1 DASH ANGOSTURA BITTERS

1 EGG WHITE

1 OUNCE CLUB SODA

ORANGE AND NUTMEG FOR GARNISH

Dry shake all ingredients except club soda, then shake again with ice. Strain into a Collins glass with ice, and top with club soda. Garnish with an orange twist and freshly grated nutmeg.

★ NOTE ★

Ron Zacapa is a rum made with virgin sugarcane honey and then aged and blended using the solera method. Used to produce vinegar, sherry, and brandy in particular, the process allows for a constant average age for a product. No container is ever fully drained. A percentage of the product in the oldest barrel is bottled. The empty space is filled from the second oldest barrel and so on.

BEE'S KISS

Sometimes cocktail names aren't terribly creative. If it mentions a bee, you can guarantee that it contains honey. Still, this is a nice after-dinner drink from the land of milk and honey for those hot Havana nights. Keep the cream in the larger half of the shaking tin until ready to give a brisk shake.

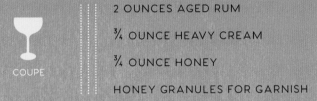

COUPE

2 OUNCES AGED RUM

¾ OUNCE HEAVY CREAM

¾ OUNCE HONEY

HONEY GRANULES FOR GARNISH

Dry shake all ingredients, then shake again with ice. Double strain into a chilled coupe. Garnish with granulated honey.

★ NOTE ★

When blackberries are in season they make a grand addition as a garnish.

MAYDAY #2

This is the second in a series of three drinks that we created that use rhubarb and Aperol. Rhubarb comes into season around the start of May, which is also when we created this delectable cocktail. The rested but unaged Neisson Blanc showcases the sugarcane, while the cucumber notes in the Bittermens Boston Bittahs bring out the fruitiness of the Aperol.

COUPE

1 OUNCE NEISSON BLANC RUM

½ OUNCE APEROL

1 OUNCE RHUBARB SYRUP (PAGE 11)

½ OUNCE LEMON JUICE

1 DASH BITTERMENS BOSTON BITTAHS

1 OUNCE DRY SPARKLING WINE

Shake all ingredients except sparkling wine with ice, and strain into a coupe. Top with sparkling wine.

★ NOTE ★

The May Day #1 appears in the PDT Cocktail Book and features gin as the base spirit. The third variation on the theme uses apple brandy.

VIOLA ROYALE

This drink tips its straw to a couple of our favorite classics: It's a little bit of a Clover Club, a little bit of an Aviation, and a little bit of a Ramos Gin Fizz. The crème de violette picks up the floral notes of the raspberries, the maraschino brings the funk, and the egg white and cream smooth it all out. It's great when everybody can be friends.

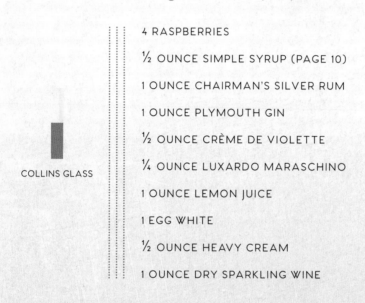

COLLINS GLASS

4 RASPBERRIES

½ OUNCE SIMPLE SYRUP (PAGE 10)

1 OUNCE CHAIRMAN'S SILVER RUM

1 OUNCE PLYMOUTH GIN

½ OUNCE CRÈME DE VIOLETTE

¼ OUNCE LUXARDO MARASCHINO

1 OUNCE LEMON JUICE

1 EGG WHITE

½ OUNCE HEAVY CREAM

1 OUNCE DRY SPARKLING WINE

In a shaker tin, muddle the raspberries in the simple syrup. Add remaining ingredients except dry sparkling wine, dry shake, and then shake with ice. Double strain into a fizz or Collins glass, and top with sparkling wine.

OLD CUBAN

Audrey Saunders, New York City's "Queen of Mixology," created this new Cuban classic at her must-visit lounge, Pegu Club, named for a colonial British officers' club in Burma. The Old Cuban—like a dressed-up Mojito (page 170)—is a sophisticated drink that has the flexibility to use other aged rums, such as Havana Club 7 Year.

FLUTE

6 MINT LEAVES

½ OUNCE DEMERARA SYRUP (PAGE 10)

1 OUNCE EL DORADO 15 YEAR RUM

1 OUNCE EL DORADO 5 YEAR RUM

½ OUNCE LIME JUICE

3 DASHES ANGOSTURA BITTERS

3 OUNCES DRY SPARKLING WINE

In a shaker tin, gently muddle mint in the demerara syrup. Add remaining ingredients except sparkling wine, and shake with ice. Double strain into a flute, and top with sparkling wine.

★ NOTE ★

Saunders's recipe calls for a garnish of sugared vanilla beans. If you can't readily find any, don't worry. The drink tastes just as good without them.

HOT CONCOCTIONS

Wherever a winter wind blows, you'll find hot alcoholic beverages. Winter nights in Cuba can slide into the mid-60s Fahrenheit, cold enough to make you want something warm to ward off the chill.

One of the New World's most popular cold-weather drinks was the loggerhead flip: rum, stout beer, and a sweetener combined in a pitcher and heated with a loggerhead, an iron ball on a long handle kept on or in the stove. Almost all taverns served the frothy, warm loggerhead flip, and historical records show price controls requiring taverns to make all flips relatively the same price. Consequently, the flip became a way for tavern keeps to distinguish their venues, adding interesting and exotic flavors to their versions of the drink. The modern-day flip (pages 83–99) bears no real relation to the loggerhead flip—other than that some tavern keeps might have used eggs in their variants—but these hot concoctions will keep you warm on a cold winter's day or night.

FOR WHAT AILS YA

Many cold-weather drinks are designed either to ward off illness or to alleviate its symptoms when that winter cold finally hits. The toddy, a cold-weather classic, is frequently made with whiskey these days, but that wasn't always the case. The name comes from the Hindi word *tari*, meaning the sap of the palmyra palm tree, which was fermented into palm wine (still a common beverage in parts of Asia and Africa). In colonial days, rum went into toddies as often as whiskey. In this Caribbean-style toddy, lemon, ginger, and cayenne provide a triple boost against what ails ya.

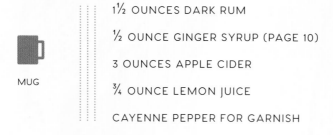

MUG

1½ OUNCES DARK RUM

½ OUNCE GINGER SYRUP (PAGE 10)

3 OUNCES APPLE CIDER

¾ OUNCE LEMON JUICE

CAYENNE PEPPER FOR GARNISH

Build all ingredients in a small pan, and bring to a boil. Pour into a mug, and garnish with a dusting of cayenne pepper.

"Published instructions for reviving victims of drowning in Massachusetts called for blowing tobacco smoke up the victim's rectum (machines were built specifically for this purpose) while bathing the victim's breast with hot rum."

—WAYNE CURTIS, *AND A BOTTLE OF RUM: A HISTORY OF THE NEW WORLD IN TEN COCKTAILS*

HOT BUTTERED RUM

This warming drink dates back to the mid-seventeenth century, when distilleries first appeared in Britain's New England colonies. Americans were making and drinking rum, and a lot of it, so it didn't take long to figure out ways to use it to stave off the cold. Toddies, nogs, and other warm cocktails all have molasses rum in them. This is a comforting drink for a blustery New England day.

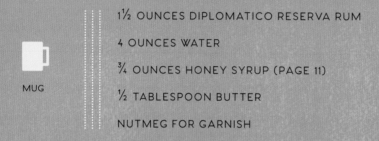

MUG

1½ OUNCES DIPLOMATICO RESERVA RUM

4 OUNCES WATER

¾ OUNCES HONEY SYRUP (PAGE 11)

½ TABLESPOON BUTTER

NUTMEG FOR GARNISH

Build all ingredients in a small pan, and bring to a boil while whisking continuously. Pour into a mug, and top liberally with fresh grated nutmeg.

MIEL PICANTE

A little sweeter than the For What Ails Ya (page 102), this drink has a different kind of bite but the same kick—its name in Spanish means "spicy honey." This spiked cider gets its jolt from the spicy honey syrup and lemon, both of which boost your immune system. See? Sometimes drinking can be good for you! Perfect for when the smell of fresh apples laces autumn winds.

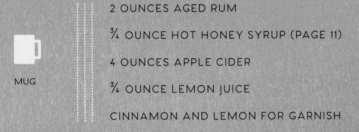

MUG

2 OUNCES AGED RUM

¾ OUNCE HOT HONEY SYRUP (PAGE 11)

4 OUNCES APPLE CIDER

¾ OUNCE LEMON JUICE

CINNAMON AND LEMON FOR GARNISH

On the stovetop, heat all ingredients together until steaming. Pour into a mug, and garnish with grated cinnamon and a lemon wedge.

ORCHARD TODDY

Pears might not grow in Cuba's tropical climate, but that doesn't mean that they don't pair well with rum. In fact, the sweetness of each complements the other—particularly when tempered with the stringency of rye whiskey—in this autumnal cocktail. Every sip is like a trip through a fragrant pear orchard.

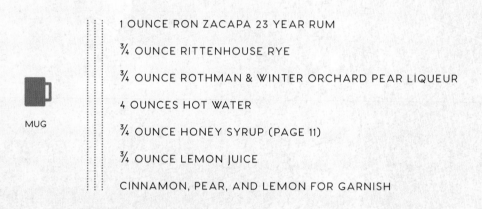

MUG

1 OUNCE RON ZACAPA 23 YEAR RUM

¾ OUNCE RITTENHOUSE RYE

¾ OUNCE ROTHMAN & WINTER ORCHARD PEAR LIQUEUR

4 OUNCES HOT WATER

¾ OUNCE HONEY SYRUP (PAGE 11)

¾ OUNCE LEMON JUICE

CINNAMON, PEAR, AND LEMON FOR GARNISH

Build all ingredients in a small pan, and bring to a boil. Pour into a mug, and top with fresh grated cinnamon and pear and lemon slices.

★ NOTE ★

Popular in the Alps as a winter lodge drink, orchard pear liqueur is an Austrian eau-de-vie made from the Williams pear, called Bartlett stateside.

BANANA SPICED RUM

Hot Buttered Rum (page 104) is a particularly New England drink, but this recipe takes it down south to the land of bananas and plantains. It takes its lead from Bananas Foster, the famous dessert created by Paul Blangé at Brennan's in New Orleans and named for Richard Foster, a friend of the owner. It's a kind of banana sundae with a sauce made of butter, brown sugar, rum, and banana liqueur. If you've never had it—and really you should—now you can have your dessert and drink it, too!

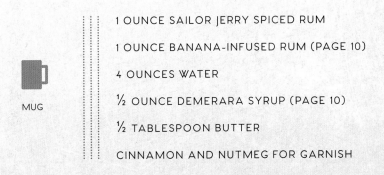

MUG

1 OUNCE SAILOR JERRY SPICED RUM

1 OUNCE BANANA-INFUSED RUM (PAGE 10)

4 OUNCES WATER

½ OUNCE DEMERARA SYRUP (PAGE 10)

½ TABLESPOON BUTTER

CINNAMON AND NUTMEG FOR GARNISH

Build ingredients in a small pan, and bring to a boil while whisking thoroughly. Pour into a mug, and top with fresh grated cinnamon and nutmeg.

★ NOTE ★

For this recipe, we recommend that you use Hamilton 151 for the infused rum.

THE CITRUS

& THE GOLDEN AGE

As the golden age dawned, the holy trinity of
Cuban cocktails—rum, lime, and sugar—
gave way to the era of famous cantineros,
the men behind the drinks.

DAIQUIRÍS

For rum and lime, it was love at first sip.

In the eighteenth century, British sailors drank rum and lots of it. But it turned out that they tended to drink the same amount of grog—rum, lime, and water—one of the earliest rum cocktails. Named for Vice Admiral Edward Vernon, known as Old Grog for the grogram coat he wore, the combination curbed rampant drunkenness at sea, but the citrus also acted as a preservative and importantly helped prevent scurvy. Since then, that delicious pairing of ingredients has pleased mariners and landlubbers alike. By the end of the nineteenth century, Bacardí had pioneered his new style of rum, and then, several decades later, Prohibition pushed American cocktail culture offshore, enshrining it in Cuba.

In its most basic form, the daiquirí contains rum, lime, and a sweetener. The word itself comes from the native Taíno people and the name of a town on the southeast coast of the country near Santiago de Cuba, a perfect place to sip this delicious drink. If you can't make it to Cuba, make sure to drink one on July 19, which is National Daiquirí Day.

EL FLORIDITA NO. 1

The Classic Daiquirí

The bar that the world knows now as El Floridita opened in 1819 as La Piña de Plata, the Silver Pineapple, originally selling fresh juice. Beverage sales boomed, a bar and restaurant joined the ranks, and in time La Piña de Plata became Bar La Florida and then El Floridita, which means "little flowery one." Under the ownership of Constantino Ribalaigua i Vert and the game-changing patronage of Ernest Hemingway, La Florida earned its reputation as *la cuna del daiquirí*—literally "the cradle of the daiquirí," but in better English, the birthplace of the legendary cocktail.

COUPE

2 OUNCES WHITE RUM

¾ OUNCE LUXARDO MARASCHINO

¾ OUNCE LIME JUICE

LIME OR BRANDIED CHERRY FOR GARNISH

Shake with ice, and strain into a chilled coupe. Garnish with a lime wheel or cherry.

EL FLORIDITA NO. 2

This variation emphasizes the citrus components of the drink.

COUPE

2 OUNCES WHITE RUM

¾ OUNCE CURAÇAO

½ OUNCE LIME JUICE

½ OUNCE ORANGE JUICE

BRANDIED CHERRY FOR GARNISH

Shake with ice, and strain into a chilled coupe. Garnish with a cherry.

LA CUNA DEL DAIQUIRÍ

"And now, Messieurs et Mesdames, the one
and only tropical daiquirí."

—CHARLES H. BAKER JR.,
THE GENTLEMAN'S COMPANION (1939)

Pinning down the history of a cocktail presents a mix of problems—the most pertinent being inebriation. Palates change, products disappear, and myths emerge into the collective consciousness. Somewhere in that mix lie the few true strands of a cocktail's origin story. The daiquirí is one of the few sours with its own identity, but that identity has several variations.

Many cocktail historians point to Jennings Cox—an American mining engineer assigned to a post near Daiquirí, Cuba—as the creator of the drink. But how did Cox make it? In a letter to the editor of *El País*, Francesco Dominico Pagliuchi, one of Cox's friends, recalled the cocktail's creation as a shaken combination of Bacardi rum, lemon, sugar, and ice—lacking the quintessential lime—that arose from necessity when, in 1898, no other ingredients were available.

A second story, from Facundo Bacardí himself, traces Jennings Cox and the creation of the daiquirí to the Venus Bar in Santiago de Cuba. The Venus Bar recipe calls for Bacardi rum, lime, sugar, and ice. But this time the ingredients are stirred over shaved ice and not strained before serving. The lemon has given way to lime, but now the drink is being stirred. Competing stories muddle history yet again.

It's hard to say which recipe was the original, but over time those changing palates, products, and myths have given us the drink we know and love today, and we do know that the daiquirí made its move from local favorite in Santiago de Cuba to Havana mainstay by way of Emilio "Maragato" Gonzalez, who first popularized the drink at the bar of the Hotel Plaza.

EL FLORIDITA NO. 3

The Hemingway Daiquirí

In the 1930s, Hemingway lived for a time in the Hotel Ambos Mundos on Havana's Calle Obispo before buying the Finca Vigía, a fifteen-acre estate about ten miles south of Old Havana. But he spent much of his time at Bar La Florida, as it was still known then. The story goes that he wanted a daiquirí with no sugar and twice the rum. Not all of us can drink like Papa, so this recipe skips the extra hard stuff. This cocktail appeared in the *Bar La Florida Cocktails* guide, published in 1935, which called the drink the "E. Henmiway" Special. The bitterness of the grapefruit nicely cuts the sweetness of the rum.

COUPE

1½ OUNCES WHITE RUM

¾ OUNCE LUXARDO MARASCHINO

1 OUNCE GRAPEFRUIT JUICE

½ OUNCE LIME JUICE

BRANDIED CHERRY FOR GARNISH

Shake with ice, and strain into a chilled coupe. Garnish with cherry.

"He was drinking another of the frozen Daiquirís with no sugar in it. . . . It reminded him of the sea. The frappéd part of the drink was like the wake of a ship and the clear part was the way the water looked when the bow cut it when you were in shallow water over marl bottom."

—ERNEST HEMINGWAY, *ISLANDS IN THE STREAM* (1970)

PAPA DOBLE

Some of us can drink like the master of modernist prose, however. This recipe is for when you want a cocktail with bite and just a hint of sweetness.

COLLINS GLASS

3 OUNCES WHITE RUM

¼ OUNCE LUXARDO MARASCHINO

3 OUNCES GRAPEFRUIT JUICE

1 OUNCE LIME JUICE

1½ CUP CRACKED ICE

GRAPEFRUIT AND BRANDIED CHERRY FOR GARNISH

Build in blender, and blend until frothy. Garnish with grapefruit slice and cherry. If you're feeling brave, whip shake the ingredients with the ice instead. Have one and have another, and you'll have a story to tell.

HEMINGWAY & CUBA

In 1938, when Ernest Hemingway's notoriety began interfering with his personal life, he left Key West and moved ninety miles south to Havana. A productive alcoholic, Hemingway completed *For Whom the Bell Tolls, Across the River and into the Trees, The Old Man and the Sea,* and *A Moveable Feast* during his time in Cuba. In time he considered himself a "Cubano sato," a garden-variety Cuban. He regularly visited Bar La Florida, where he instructed El Constante in the creation of what became the Papa Doble (page 119), which he consumed while standing because "you can drink more that way." Hemingway's record was fifteen consumed in one standing. It had "no taste of alcohol and felt, as you drank them, the way downhill glacier skiing feels running through powder snow." When El Constante wrote the Bar La Florida cocktail book, he returned the ingredients to their original proportions. Toward the end of his time in Cuba, Hemingway had become a prickly drunk plied with booze by a lackey, obsessed with his virility, and easily provoked into violent rages. His personal turmoil foretold the political unrest about to overtake the island. But for more than twenty years, Hemingway was an integral part of Cuba, and his legacy continues. Today, a whole Hemingway industry exists there. A statue of him stands in his regular spot in the corner of El Floridita, and his home outside Havana has become a museum.

EL FLORIDITA NO. 4

The Frozen Daiquirí

This slightly sweeter variation of the daiquirí uses simple syrup that balances the tartness of the lime juice and the maraschino liqueur. Maraschino is distilled from marasca cherries—which hail originally from the coast of Croatia—not to be confused with those neon red cherry monsters. Luxardo is one of the best brands of maraschino liqueur.

COUPE

2 OUNCES WHITE RUM

¼ OUNCE LUXARDO MARASCHINO

½ OUNCE SIMPLE SYRUP (PAGE 10)

¾ OUNCE LIME JUICE

1 CUP ICE

LIME FOR GARNISH

Blend at high speed for 15 seconds, and strain into a chilled coupe. Garnish with a lime wheel. This drink is also delicious shaken over ice, as shown here.

"My mojito in La Bodeguita, my daiquirí in El Floridita."

—ERNEST HEMINGWAY

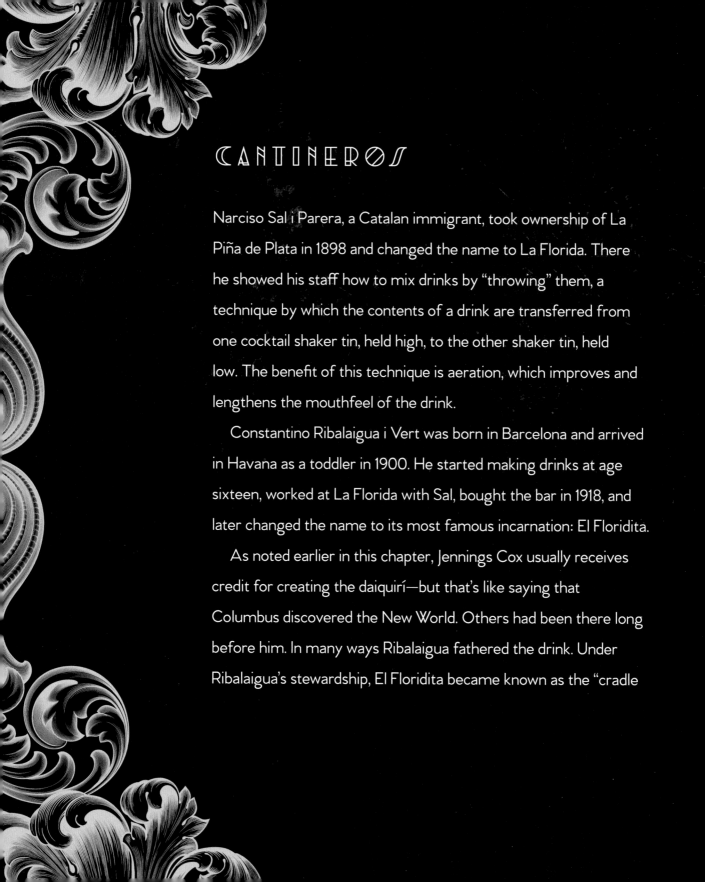

CANTINEROS

Narciso Sal i Parera, a Catalan immigrant, took ownership of La Piña de Plata in 1898 and changed the name to La Florida. There he showed his staff how to mix drinks by "throwing" them, a technique by which the contents of a drink are transferred from one cocktail shaker tin, held high, to the other shaker tin, held low. The benefit of this technique is aeration, which improves and lengthens the mouthfeel of the drink.

Constantino Ribalaigua i Vert was born in Barcelona and arrived in Havana as a toddler in 1900. He started making drinks at age sixteen, worked at La Florida with Sal, bought the bar in 1918, and later changed the name to its most famous incarnation: El Floridita.

As noted earlier in this chapter, Jennings Cox usually receives credit for creating the daiquirí—but that's like saying that Columbus discovered the New World. Others had been there long before him. In many ways Ribalaigua fathered the drink. Under Ribalaigua's stewardship, El Floridita became known as the "cradle of the daiquirí," and Constantino became known as "El Constante" for his constant presence at the bar. He always arrived early to prepare for the new day and never left before the last of his guests departed. Ribalaigua shrewdly understood that he needed a hook to make his bar into something more than just a local watering hole. In 1925, he acquired an electric blender, and the Floridita No. 4, mixed "en frappe," was born. Through his endless experimentation and the presence of his legendary regular Ernest Hemingway, firmly planted in the corner of the bar, Ribalaigua made the daiquirí synonymous with the golden age of Cuban cocktails.

Emilio "Maragato" Gonzalez, a contemporary of Ribalaigua, popularized Cuban cocktails with the elite clientele of the bars at Hotel Florida and Hotel Plaza. With Ribalaigua, he also cofounded the Asociación de Cantineros de Cuba in 1924, nine years before the United Kingdom Bartenders Guild (often credited, incorrectly, as the world's first bartenders' association).

EL FLORIDITA NO. 5

The Pink Daiquirí

In the days when Facundo Bacardí y Massó was refining his distillation recipe for Cuban rum, he gave his workers a mixture of rum, sugar, and lemon or lime. In the early twentieth century, grenadine joined the mix, and the drink became known as the Bacardi Cocktail. At the time, Bacardi was the world's leading rum and a proprietary eponym—the term used when a brand name becomes so widespread that it can lose the legal protection of being trademarked. To avoid that fate, Bacardí took the unprecedented step of suing the Barbizon Plaza Hotel and Wivel's Restaurant, both in New York City, for not using Bacardi rum in a Bacardi Cocktail. The New York Supreme Court ruled in Bacardí's favor, ensuring that using the company's name meant that no one could use another brand of rum. When the Bacardi Cocktail began to fall out of favor, Bacardí tried to rename the cocktail the Grenadine Daiquirí, but the new name never stuck.

This variation of the Floridita bears a striking resemblance to the Bacardi Cocktail but adds a matching amount of maraschino liqueur to cut the sweetness of the grenadine.

COUPE

2 OUNCES WHITE RUM

¼ OUNCE LUXARDO MARASCHINO

¼ OUNCE GRENADINE (PAGE 10)

¾ OUNCE LIME JUICE

Shake with ice, and strain into a chilled coupe. Garnish optionally with a brandied cherry.

★ NOTE ★

You don't need to use Bacardi rum for this drink. Feel free to use any good white rum without fear of legal repercussions.

BROOKLYNITE

During the Ten Years' War (1868–1878), freedom fighters in the Captaincy General of Cuba drank a combination of honey, aguardiente—any locally distilled liquor, literally "fire water"—and citrus. They called the mixture a Canchanchara, and during that unsuccessful struggle for independence cavalry officers often had a bottle slung from their saddles. Like the Cuba Libre but less well known outside the island nation, the Canchanchara has become synonymous with the Cuban struggle for independence. Honoring that traditional combination of citrus, honey, and rum, the Brooklynite comes from the *Stork Club Bar Book* by Lucius Beebe (1946).

COUPE

2 OUNCES JAMAICAN RUM

¾ OUNCE HONEY SYRUP (PAGE 11)

1 OUNCE LIME JUICE

1 DASH ANGOSTURA BITTERS

LIME FOR GARNISH

Shake with ice, and strain into a chilled coupe. Garnish with a lime wheel.

CIENFUEGOS SHAKE

Traditionally, a "shake" consists of a dark spirit, such as bourbon or cognac, plus lime and sugar. For this drink, a heavily aged rum serves as the spirit base, and the Bénédictine provides a sweet, honeyed note. Frenchman Alexandre Le Grande created the herbal liqueur from a closely guarded combination of botanicals in the 1860s—although for marketing purposes he claimed that monks at the Benedictine Abbey of Fécamp in Normandy had produced the mixture during the French Revolution. This is a sturdy rum cocktail for anyone who enjoys a good whiskey sour.

COUPE

6 MINT LEAVES

¾ OUNCE SIMPLE SYRUP (PAGE 10)

2 OUNCES EL DORADO 15 YEAR OLD RUM

½ OUNCE BÉNÉDICTINE

1 OUNCE LIME JUICE

3 DASHES ANGOSTURA BITTERS

In shaker tin, muddle mint with simple syrup. Add remaining ingredients to the tin, shake with ice, and double strain into a chilled coupe.

"Cienfuegos es la ciudad que más me gusta a mí."

—BENY MORÉ

HONEYSUCKLE

Although David Embury, a New York City tax lawyer, had "never been engaged in any of the manifold branches of the liquor business," he had very strong opinions about cocktails. In 1948 Doubleday published his book, *The Fine Art of Mixing Drinks*, which advises that you can transform the Honeysuckle into the Honey Bee by using a dark rum, which adds a certain brashness—sting, if you like—to the drink.

COUPE

2 OUNCES WHITE RUM

¾ OUNCE HONEY SYRUP (PAGE 11)

¾ OUNCE LIME JUICE

Shake with ice, and strain into a chilled coupe. Garnish with a lime wheel.

★ NOTE ★

This recipe represents our version of a Canchanchara, pictured here, which Ricardo at Café Madrigal served to us on the rocks in a rocks glass. Here are the Café Madrigal ingredients:

2 ounces white rum
¾ ounce honey syrup (page 11)
¾ ounce lemon juice

CAPTAIN'S BLOOD

This classic cocktail clearly demonstrates the transformative powers of bitters. Its origins remain fairly murky, however. Perhaps it has something to do with Errol Flynn, who made his Hollywood debut in a leading role as the title character in *Captain Blood* in 1935. Flynn first visited Havana on his honeymoon the next year. The story goes that he stranded Lili Damita, his new bride, on his yacht so she couldn't interfere with his shenanigans in the local whorehouses. Nor was that the last of his misconduct. Soon a Havana regular, Flynn habitually threw lavish dinner parties but left the tab for his guests. Hemingway once raged: "Any picture in which Errol Flynn is the best actor is its own worst enemy." But don't let the actor's bad behavior dissuade you from trying this delicious drink.

COUPE

2 OUNCES JAMAICAN RUM

¾ OUNCES SIMPLE SYRUP (PAGE 10)

1 OUNCE LIME JUICE

2 DASHES ANGOSTURA BITTERS

Shake with ice, and strain into a chilled coupe. Garnish optionally with a lime wheel.

MULATA DAIQUIRÍ

Originally made with Bacardi Elixir, which infused rum with plums. Bacardí trademarked that liqueur in 1927, but the company no longer makes it—not to be confused with the 2011 rum of the same name made with roasted sugarcane. When Castro nationalized Bacardi's Cuban holdings in 1960, production of the liqueur ceased. Most cocktail historians believe that Ribalaigua created the Mulata, but Héctor Zumbado y Argueta, author of *El Sexto Sentido del Barman* (The Barman's Sixth Sense), credits José Maria Vazquez with creating it at the Hotel Lincoln in the 1940s.

COUPE

1½ OUNCES EL DORADO 5 YEAR RUM

¾ OUNCE TEMPUS FUGIT CRÈME DE CACAO

¾ OUNCE LIME JUICE

1 BARSPOON CANE SYRUP

Shake with ice, and strain into a chilled coupe.

★ NOTE ★

This drink is rare in America, but in Cuba it holds court among the more popular daiquirís on many cocktail menus and appears in almost all of Havana Club's marketing materials.

CLOAK & DAGGER

The split base of this cocktail allows a dark rum—the cloak—and a light rum—the dagger—to interact and form a flavor profile entirely different from a medium body rum mixed with the same secondary ingredients.

COUPE

1 OUNCE GOSLING'S BLACK SEAL RUM

1 OUNCE RHUM BARBANCOURT 4 YEAR

¾ OUNCE SIMPLE SYRUP (PAGE 10)

¾ OUNCE LIME JUICE

LIME FOR GARNISH

Shake with ice, and strain into a chilled coupe. Garnish with a lime wheel.

"Where we find rum, we find action, sometimes cruel, sometimes heroic, sometimes humorous, but always vigorous and interesting."

—CHARLES WILLIAM TAUSSIG,
PRESIDENT OF THE AMERICAN MOLASSES COMPANY,
RUM, ROMANCE, AND REBELLION (1928)

SOURS

The sour is a big, brave, beautiful category of drinks: one part sweet, one part sour, and two parts strong. The name can sound a little misleading, though. Sourness isn't necessarily the dominant flavor. Think of the drinks in this chapter as concentrated punches that came along after the cocktail glass overtook the punch bowl in popularity. These cocktails aim for a balance between all of their elements, which have a long, delicious history of working together.

SWEATER WEATHER

This drink—named for the weather that inspired it—is one part Hot Toddy served cold and one part Dark and Stormy. Try it during the first few weeks of spring, when there's still a lingering winter bite in the air, or as summer gives way to fall and the nights bring a hint of the coming chill. This Cienfuegos original, created by Jessica Wholers, has been on the menu since fall 2014. Despite its name, this drink is refreshing year round.

ROCKS GLASS

1½ OUNCES EL DORADO 12 YEAR RUM

¾ OUNCE RITTENHOUSE RYE

½ OUNCE COINTREAU

½ OUNCE GINGER SYRUP (PAGE 10)

¾ OUNCE LEMON JUICE

LEMON FOR GARNISH

Shake with ice, and strain into rocks glass with ice. Garnish with a lemon twist.

★ NOTE ★

For added presentation pizzazz, stud the lemon twist with whole cloves as pictured here.

ARCO DE TRIUNFO

In Parque José Martí, you'll find the Cienfuegos Arco de Triunfo (triumphal arch), a modest but meaningful monument that celebrates Cuba's independence from America in 1902. This drink is a variation of the Champs Élysées, a classic cocktail from the 1930 *Savoy Cocktail Book* by Harry Craddock, who founded the United Kingdom Bartenders Guild several years later. For this version, rum replaces the cognac. The original Savoy recipe didn't specify green or yellow chartreuse, but we tried it both ways and green means go.

COUPE

1½ OUNCES APPLETON V/X RUM

½ OUNCE GREEN CHARTREUSE

½ OUNCE SIMPLE SYRUP (PAGE 10)

¾ OUNCE LEMON JUICE

2 DASHES ANGOSTURA BITTERS

LEMON FOR GARNISH

Shake with ice, and strain into a chilled coupe. Garnish with a lemon twist.

★ NOTE ★

The text on the triumphal arch reads:

20 DE MAYO 1902
LOS OBREROS DE CIENFUEGOS A LA REPUBLICA CUBANA

May 20, 1902
From the Workers of Cienfuegos to the Cuban Republic

PENINSULA SOUR

This rum-based ode to the New York Sour needs a full-bodied rum to provide a similar heaviness as the whiskey in the original drink and is named for the Peninsula Hotel on 55th and Fifth. But this elegant and frothy concoction also pays tribute to La Punta, the small peninsula of Cienfuegos that juts out into the surrounding bay.

ROCKS GLASS

2 OUNCES BRUGAL EXTRA VIEJO RUM

¾ OUNCE SIMPLE SYRUP (PAGE 10)

¾ OUNCE LEMON JUICE

1 EGG WHITE

FRUITY RED WINE, PREFERABLY PINOT NOIR

Dry shake all ingredients except red wine to emulsify, then shake again with ice to chill and dilute. Strain into rocks glass with ice, float red wine on top, and garnish optionally with an orange and lemon twist.

> ★ NOTE ★
>
> *The different densities of the parts of this drink create a nice layered effect. Make it when you want to impress.*

ONE HUNDRED FIRES

Camilo Cienfuegos fought alongside Castro against Batista's forces, and the people of Cuba loved him as much as they loved Castro—if not more so. On January 8, 1959, when Castro entered Havana, the island's new leader announced that he was turning military barracks into a school and then asked Cienfuegos, "¿Voy bien, Camilo?" (Am I doing OK?), to which Cienfuegos replied: "Vas bien, Fidel" (You're doing fine). Cienfuegos died in a plane crash at age twenty-seven, spurring numerous conspiracy theories about the circumstances of his death and ensuring his cultural immortality in Cuba. The hellfire bitters and the flaming chili pepper in this cocktail pay homage to the hundred fires of his name, while the sweetness of the pineapple juice tempers the heat.

ROCKS GLASS

¾ OUNCE APPLE BRANDY

¾ OUNCE SANTA TERESA 1796 RUM

½ OUNCE CHILI SYRUP (PAGE 10)

¾ OUNCE LEMON JUICE

½ OUNCE PINEAPPLE JUICE

2 DASHES HELLFIRE BITTERS

CHILI PEPPER FOR GARNISH

151 RUM FOR PRESENTATION

Whip shake all ingredients, and pour into a double rocks glass filled with crushed ice. Garnish with half a chili pepper filled with the 151, and set overproof rum on fire.

THE TWENTIETH CENTURY CLUB

Few cocktails have the honor of summing up an entire century's worth of drinks, and the Twentieth Century isn't one of them. The New York Central Railroad ran a train line, called the Twentieth Century Limited, back and forth across the thousand miles between Manhattan and Chicago. This variant of the drink, named for the luxury service, uses rum instead of gin—another fine example of rum's ability to elevate a classic—while the citrus-forward Lillet Blanc enhances the tropical notes in the rich Tempus Fugit.

PUNCH GLASS

1 OUNCE RON DEL BARRILITO

¾ OUNCE LILLET BLANC

¾ OUNCE TEMPUS FUGIT CRÈME DE CACAO

¾ OUNCE LEMON JUICE

LEMON FOR GARNISH

Shake with ice, and strain into punch glass. Garnish with a lemon wheel.

★ NOTE ★

Tempus Fugit—which means "time flies" in Latin—sources cacao from Venezuela and vanilla from Mexico, paying deference to the original sources of the finest ingredients for crèmes de cacao found in nineteenth-century recipes.

BITTERSWEET SYMPHONY

A pear and rosemary pie served as the inspiration for this drink. When you combine pear with the savory notes of the rosemary and the sweetness of the rum, Bärenjäger, and syrup, you get this delicious sour. Bärenjäger, which means "bear hunter" in German, is a honey liqueur.

COUPE

2 SPRIGS ROSEMARY

¾ OUNCE DEMERARA SYRUP (PAGE 10)

1 OUNCE EL DORADO 12 YEAR OLD RUM

¾ OUNCE ORCHARD PEAR LIQUEUR

⅜ OUNCE BÄRENJÄGER

¾ OUNCE LEMON JUICE

SALT FOR GARNISH

Gently muddle 1 sprig of rosemary in the syrup. Build remaining ingredients, shake with ice, and double strain into chilled coupe. Garnish with rosemary, and sprinkle with salt.

★ NOTE ★

This cocktail pairs perfectly with the 1997 song of the same name by Britpop band The Verve.

DECEMBER MORN

This is the lovechild of a September Morn and Jack Rose, both from the *Savoy Cocktail Book*. The September Morn is a close relative of the better known Clover Club Cocktail, both red fruit sours. The Clover Club relies on raspberries for its pink hue and lighter flavor, while grenadine gives the September Morn its richer flavor and color. Ernest Hemingway helped popularize the Jack Rose, which also includes grenadine, by featuring it in *The Sun Also Rises*.

COUPE

1½ OUNCES FLOR DE CAÑA EXTRA DRY 4 YEAR RUM

½ OUNCE LAIRD'S APPLEJACK

¾ OUNCE GRENADINE (PAGE 10)

½ OUNCE LEMON JUICE

1 EGG WHITE

CINNAMON FOR GARNISH

Dry shake all ingredients without ice; then shake again with ice. Strain into chilled coupe. Grate fresh cinnamon on top.

★ NOTE ★

The word "grenadine" comes from grenade, the French word for "pomegranate." It doesn't appear in any recipes in Jerry Thomas's How to Mix Drinks (1862), but the Savoy Cocktail Book (1930) includes nearly 100 cocktails that feature it. Don't confuse the grenadine in this cocktail with the cloying mixture of sugar water, coloring, and preservatives made by a company that also sells sweetened lime juice.

DERNIER MOT

At the Detroit Athletic Club bar, Frank Fogarty, a vaudeville performer, created what has become a timeless cocktail, the Last Word. In this Caribbean variation on that classic, the gin is replaced by a rhum agricole. The French-style rum—which gives the drink's name its French twist—is distilled from fresh sugarcane instead of molasses, which gives the spirit its vibrant fruit and grassy notes. Each of the four ingredients in this recipe is a heavy hitter that can stand up to the rest.

COUPE

¾ OUNCE GREEN CHARTREUSE

¾ OUNCE LA FAVORITE BLANC AGRICOLE RHUM

¾ OUNCE LUXARDO MARASCHINO

¾ OUNCE LIME JUICE

Shake with ice, and strain into a chilled coupe.

PERIODISTA

Ernest Hemingway might have enjoyed this classic Cuban cocktail, whose name means "journalist" in Spanish. Journalists in Miami and Havana might have drunk it in excess during the Cuban missile crisis. It's hard to say because it's hard to pin down the origin story of the drink. Further complicating matters, this drink sometimes appears as a variation of the Palmetto, made with rum, vermouth, and bitters.

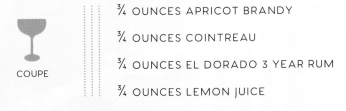

COUPE

¾ OUNCES APRICOT BRANDY

¾ OUNCES COINTREAU

¾ OUNCES EL DORADO 3 YEAR RUM

¾ OUNCES LEMON JUICE

Shake with ice, and strain into a chilled coupe. Garnish optionally with a lemon twist.

BERRY DANGEROUS FIX

Woodland strawberries served as the inspiration for this delicious drink. They're small—only the size of your fingernail—but much more flavorful and floral than the traditional variety at your local grocery store. Like the strawberries that also grow in Cuba, the woodland kind are delicate and don't travel well. But several dashes of orange flower water allow you to enjoy the taste of these berries year round.

ROCKS GLASS

3 STRAWBERRIES

½ OUNCE CANE SYRUP

1½ OUNCES PLANTATION 3 STAR WHITE RUM

¼ OUNCE CAMPARI

¾ OUNCE LEMON JUICE

3 DASHES ORANGE FLOWER WATER

LEMON FOR GARNISH

In a shaking tin, muddle 2 of the strawberries in cane syrup; then build the rest of the ingredients. Dry shake, pour into a double rocks glass, and top with crushed ice. Garnish with the third strawberry and a lemon wheel. Serve with a straw.

SOUTHERN SMITH & CROSS

People have been gazing at the constellation Crux, commonly called the Southern Cross, for many centuries. In the time of the Roman Empire, astronomer and mathematician Claudius Ptolemy classified it as a part of the constellation Centaurus, but João Faras, astronomer to King Manuel I of Portugal, receives credit for first describing it accurately in 1500. This cocktail blends two older recipes named after the constellation, one from Williams Schmidt's *The Flowing Bowl* (1891) and the other from Elsa af Trolle's *Cocktails* (1927). Think of it as a darker, funkier margarita.

COUPE

1½ OUNCES SMITH & CROSS RUM

¼ OUNCE GRAND MARNIER

½ OUNCE DEMERARA SYRUP (PAGE 10)

½ OUNCE LIME JUICE

Shake with ice, and strain into a chilled coupe.

For completists, here are the ingredients lists from the older recipes:

SOUTHERN CROSS

COUPE

Flowing Bowl version	*Cocktails* version
THE JUICE OF A LIME	THE JUICE OF 1 LEMON
A DASH MINERAL WATER	DASH SODA WATER
A SPOONFUL OF SUGAR	A TABLESPOON OF SUGAR
⅔ OF ST. CROIX RUM	⅔ ST. CROIX RUM (CRUZAN)
⅓ OF BRANDY	⅓ OF COGNAC
1 DASH OF CURAÇAO	1 DASH OF ORANGE CURAÇAO

DUTCHIE

Smith & Cross is a traditional Jamaican rum with distinct flavors that made Jamaican rum famous in the late nineteenth and early twentieth centuries. Genever is a precursor to modern gin; as such, it's a throwback, but it's been making a resurgence in recent years. Both of these rather old-fashioned styles of spirits have bold flavors, but they balance each other out.

WINE GLASS

¾ OUNCE BOLS GENEVER

¾ OUNCE SMITH & CROSS RUM

¾ OUNCE YELLOW CHARTREUSE

¾ OUNCE LIME JUICE

1 BARSPOON CANE SYRUP

½ OUNCE CLUB SODA

PEYCHAUD'S BITTERS

MINT LEAVES FOR GARNISH

Swizzle all ingredients except club soda and bitters with crushed ice in a wine glass. Top with club soda and Peychaud's bitters to taste. Garnish with mint.

★ NOTE ★

Smith & Cross, a bartender favorite, has a super-funky taste profile: Think bandages, burning tires, and rotting fruit—but delicious. It's also 114 proof, so tread carefully.

CATAMARAN

The island of Curaçao lies off the coast of Venezuela in the southern Caribbean Sea. Spanish settlers found that sugarcane didn't grow well on this desert island and instead planted Valencia orange trees. Those didn't do well either: The sandy soil made the oranges extremely bitter. Locals called the bitter fruits *larahas*—a corruption of *naranjas*, Spanish for "oranges"—but in 1771 chemist Hieronymus Gaubius noticed the aromatic qualities of the oils from larahas peels. By this time, the Dutch had won their independence from the Spanish and began settling the island in earnest. Colonists dried the peels and preserved them in rum to ship back to Holland. There, distillers macerated them into Curaçao liqueur. The slight bitterness of Curaçao works well with the nutty orgeat and references the mai tai, a tiki classic.

ROCKS GLASS

¾ OUNCE APPLETON V/X RUM

¾ OUNCE BEEFEATER GIN

¼ OUNCE CURAÇAO

½ OUNCE ORGEAT (PAGE 11)

¾ OUNCE LIME JUICE

PINEAPPLE FOR GARNISH

Whip shake, and strain into a double rocks glass filled with crushed ice. Garnish with a pineapple slice.

RUBY RUM

This is Hemingway's beloved daiquirí, reworked into a swizzle, in which Aperol—an Italian aperitif made with bitter orange, cinchona (the tree that gives us quinine), rhubarb, and other ingredients—replaces the maraschino liqueur. The grapefruit juice highlights the drink's delicate bitterness, reined in by the full-bodied Gosling's and herbal mint notes.

SWIZZLE GLASS

1 OUNCE APEROL

1 OUNCE GOSLING'S BLACK SEAL RUM

½ OUNCE MINT SYRUP (PAGE 11)

½ OUNCE GRAPEFRUIT JUICE

½ OUNCE LIME JUICE

MINT LEAVES FOR GARNISH

Swizzle all ingredients with crushed ice in a swizzle glass, and garnish with mint.

★ NOTE ★

James Gosling left England in 1806, bound for America, then still a fledgling nation. He set up shop in Bermuda, however, and founded the company that still bears his name. In 1863, Gosling released its first Old Rum, distributing it in barrels to people who brought their own bottles, which were sealed in black wax, which gave the product its new name.

MIND IF I DO JULEP

Although technically not a swizzle, this drink requires a similar technique (ingredients mixed over crushed ice) and results in an equal amount of refreshment. In the 1700s the julep was predominantly a rum drink. After the Revolutionary War, it transitioned to whiskey, followed by brandy in more prosperous times. The mint remains the common factor. Later, many juleps featured the addition of a rum float—"controversial" according to the always opinionated David Embury. The Mind If I Do Julep embraces that tradition but reverses it by adding a float of Laird's Applejack to a rum julep.

JULEP CUP

2 OUNCES BARBANCOURT 8 YEAR RUM

½ OUNCE BUFFALO TRACE BOURBON

¼ OUNCE CANE SYRUP

¼ OUNCE LAIRD'S APPLEJACK

MINT LEAVES FOR GARNISH

Swizzle all ingredients except applejack with crushed ice in a julep cup. Float applejack on top, and garnish with mint.

★ NOTE ★

Like many alcoholic beverages, especially those featuring mint, the julep originally served as a medicinal treatment for stomach ailments.

MARTINIQUE SWIZZLE

Swizzle stick trees grow abundantly on Martinique, where swizzle sticks are called *baton-lele*. This cocktail is a great way to showcase a classic rum and the importance of technique. The ingredients make it seem similar to a daiquiri, but swizzling aerates and dilutes differently than shaking, so the elements taste brighter and fresher.

SWIZZLE GLASS

2 OUNCES SAINT JAMES AMBER RUM

½ OUNCE CANE SYRUP

½ OUNCE LIME JUICE

1 DASH ABSINTHE

1 DASH ANGOSTURA BITTERS

MINT LEAVES FOR GARNISH

Swizzle all ingredients with crushed ice in a swizzle glass. Garnish with mint.

"Swizzles originated in the West Indies, where everything, including hot chocolate, is swizzled. A swizzle stick is the branch of a tropical bush with three to five forked branches on the end. You insert this in the glass or pitcher and twirl the stem rapidly between the palms of your hands. By rapid swizzling with fine ice, you'll get a good outside frost."

—TRADER VIC'S BARTENDER'S GUIDE

ARRACK SWIZZLE

Batavia—the Roman name for part of what became the Netherlands and the Dutch colonial name for Jakarta—was the capital of the Dutch East Indies until the Japanese invaded in 1942 and renamed the city Jakarta. Arrack is a liquor made in Southeast Asia from sugarcane and fermented red rice. Batavia arrack has been made since the seventeenth century, and its powerful, funky flavor was a must in classic punch recipes. Here that power is kept in check by the Chairman's Reserve rum.

WINE GLASS

1 OUNCE BATAVIA ARRACK

¾ OUNCE CHAIRMAN'S RESERVE RUM

¾ OUNCE COCCHI SWEET VERMOUTH

½ OUNCE CANE SYRUP

¾ OUNCE LEMON JUICE

6 DASHES ANGOSTURA BITTERS

MINT FOR GARNISH

Swizzle all ingredients except bitters with crushed ice in a wine glass. Top with bitters, and garnish with a mint sprig.

QUEEN'S PARK SWIZZLE

The Queen's Park is a hotel on the island of Trinidad that boasted poor accommodations but a good bar, the Long Bar with the Brass Rail. The original recipe called for a dark, heavy demerara rum, probably because Trinidad wasn't producing its own rum when this drink was created. Demerara rum came from nearby Guyana, but a lighter rum serves as a better vehicle for the flavors of the lime and bitters.

SWIZZLE GLASS

12–15 MINT LEAVES

¾ OUNCE SIMPLE SYRUP (PAGE 10)

2 OUNCES LIGHT RUM

1 OUNCE LIME JUICE

ANGOSTURA BITTERS

PEYCHAUD'S BITTERS

MINT LEAVES FOR GARNISH

In a swizzle glass, muddle mint in the syrup. Add rum and lime juice, and swizzle with crushed ice. Top with Angostura and Peychaud's bitters to taste, and garnish with mint.

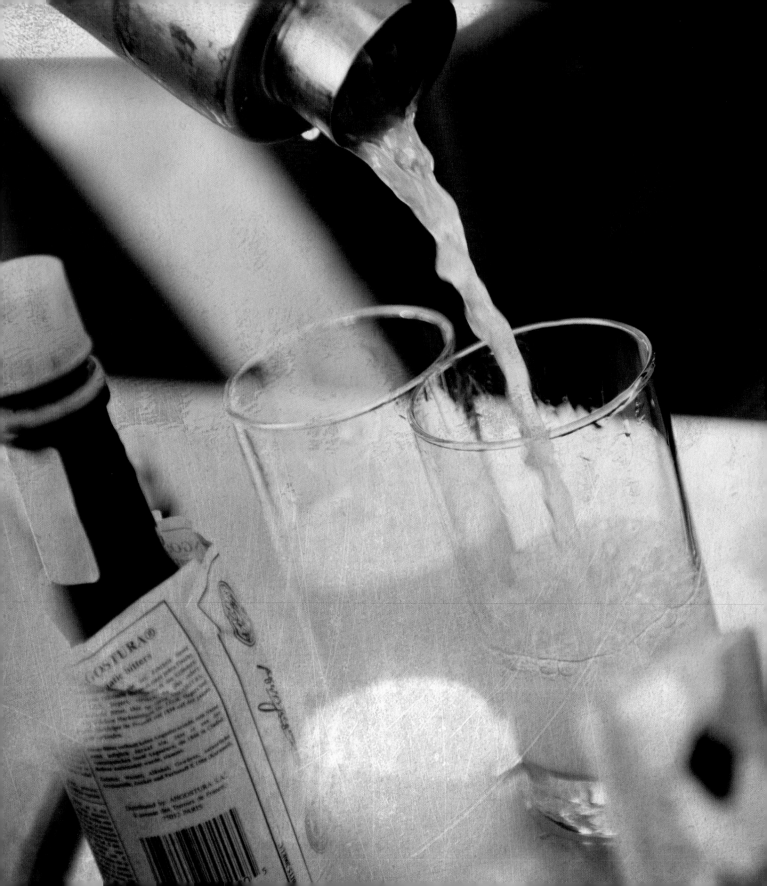

RICKEYS & OTHER HIGHBALLS

The highball is a family of mixed drinks in which the base spirit combines with a non-alcoholic mixer, often club soda. It might seem strange to us today, but for most of the nineteenth century the idea of diluting a perfectly good spirit with club soda was crazy talk. Thankfully, tastes change. The rickey takes its name from Joe Rickey, a southern lobbyist who popularized the whiskey version in Washington, D.C., during the 1880s. But the drink gained widespread popularity about a decade later when made with gin. At that same time, bartender Patrick Gavin Duffy, who later wrote the *Official Mixer's Manual* (1934), was making highballs in New York. (Using railroad terminology, the word originally referred to how fast the drink could be made.) Broadly, a rickey uses lime juice while a Collins uses lemon juice.

MOJITO

In 1950, Angel Martinez officially changed the name of his bodega from Casa Martinez to La Bodeguita del Medio, and by then he was already well known for his Mojito Criollo ("little Creole citrus mixture" in Spanish). The bartenders there receive credit for first muddling the mint in the drink. Whether first enjoyed off the coast of Havana aboard Sir Francis Drake's ship (page 172) or crafted by the skillful hands of cantineros past and present, the mojito is an iconic Cuban cocktail.

COLLINS GLASS

6 MINT LEAVES, PLUS ADDITIONAL FOR GARNISH

¾ OUNCE SIMPLE SYRUP (PAGE 10)

2 OUNCES WHITE RUM

¾ OUNCE LIME JUICE

CLUB SODA

In a shaker tin, muddle the mint leaves in simple syrup. Add rum and lime juice. Whip shake with crushed ice, and strain into a Collins glass filled with ice cubes. Top with club soda, and garnish with mint.

Bartenders make the drink a little differently in Cuba. Muddle 1 heaping barspoon superfine sugar, 12 mint leaves, and 1 ounce lime juice in a Collins glass. Add 2 ounces club soda, swizzle, fill with ice cubes, and top with rum.

★ NOTE ★

If you can find it, Havana Club 3 Year Rum is best for making mojitos. See page 174 for more on Havana Club.

THE PROTO-MOJITO

The precursor to the mojito was probably the Draque, possibly created by Sir Francis Drake, his cousin Richard Drake, or his nephew Sir Richard Hawkins, perhaps to mask the unpleasant odors and flavors of aguardiente or to relieve a stomach ailment.

In 1585, Queen Elizabeth I of England signed a treaty with the Dutch, a move that her former brother-in-law, King Philip II of Spain, took as a declaration of war since the Netherlands belonged to the Spanish crown at the time. The next year, in a preemptive strike, Elizabeth sent Drake on his Great Expedition to attack Spanish colonies in the New World. (Returning the favor, King Philip purportedly put a bounty of 20,000 ducats—more than $6 million today—on Sir Francis's head.) Drake's fleet intended to sack Havana before returning to England, but his crew fell ill, and he abandoned the plan.

Mint has always been used as a remedy for stomach disorders, and we know that Drake's ships sailed with aguardiente on them. Today, many of the Spanish ports that Drake hit on his Great Expedition feature drinks similar to the Draque, whether existing before he got there or arising afterward. In Maracaibo, Venezuela, a *draque* is an aguardiente-based stomach remedy. In Mexico, the *drage* is an energetic herbal tisane. In Cartagena, Colombia, it offers relief from dehydration.

The Draque began transforming into the mojito at a beach bar called La Concha in Marianao, Cuba. The Concha Mojito was basically a Ron Collins, with rum, lemon juice, sugar, Angostura bitters, and club soda. The 1935 *Bar La Florida* cocktail guide features a Mojito Criollo that drops the Angostura bitters and includes mint, but La Bodeguita del Medio (shown below) remains most well known for popularizing the tropical classic.

HAVANA CLUB

The Arechabala family began producing Havana Club rum in Cárdenas, Cuba, in 1878, around the same time that the Bacardí family first started distilling in Santiago de Cuba. José Arechabala y Aldama established the company, but his grandnephew, José Iturrioz y Llaguno, created the new mythical product.

Iturrioz took over the company in 1926, when Cárdenas was stalling in a severe economic depression due largely to the shallowness of its port, which redirected business to Havana and Matanzas. Iturrioz marshaled engineers, equipment, and the manpower needed to dredge the harbor and construct the Espigón (breakwater) in 1939. For four years, countless Cardenenses carried out this monumental task.

By 1944 the job was complete and Cárdenas also had a new shoreline with a new marina, seaside road, esplanade, green spaces, and a monument commemorating the first time the Cuban flag flew on Cuban soil. By the late 1950s, the Arechabala family was producing not only Havana Club rum but also Relicario brandy, Arechabala creams, Quirnal vermouth, Arechabala Cognac, Caña Rum, and candy. After the revolution, Castro's government nationalized the distillery. The Arechabala family fled to Spain and allowed the trademark to lapse in 1973.

The Cuban government partnered with Pernod-Ricard in 1993 to produce the "original" Havana Club, which it claimed as its own. The next year Bacardi partnered with the Arechabalas and then a few years later bought the family's residual rights to the Havana Club brand, including the original distillation recipe. The legal battle between the two spirits giants for recognition of the official trademark continues today amid the ongoing trade embargo.

SOLERA BUCK

A buck is a drink made with ginger beer. This drink is a little Dark & Stormy plus a little Moscow Mule, minus any brand affiliations. The Dark & Stormy became popular on the British island of Bermuda, made using Gosling's dark, funky, and sweet molasses rum. After 1860, the Royal Navy began making its own ginger beer, around the time that the Dark & Stormy was invented. Originally yeast gave the ginger beverage its fizz. For this drink, the ginger appears in the form of a syrup, and club soda brings the fizz.

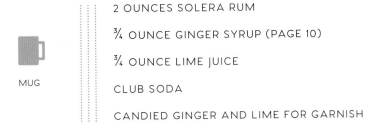

2 OUNCES SOLERA RUM

¾ OUNCE GINGER SYRUP (PAGE 10)

¾ OUNCE LIME JUICE

CLUB SODA

CANDIED GINGER AND LIME FOR GARNISH

MUG

Shake all ingredients except club soda with ice, and strain into a copper mug filled with ice. Top with club soda, and garnish with candied ginger and a lime wheel.

> ★ NOTE ★
>
> *Gosling's holds the trademark to the Dark & Stormy cocktail, which means, if you order the drink by that name, it must contain Gosling's rum.*

CUBA LIBRE

Rupert Grant—a calypso songwriter from the island of Trinidad better known by his *nom de chanson*, Lord Invader—originally penned the song "Rum and Coca-Cola" about American soldiers and their off-duty activities. The Andrews Sisters' 1945 version of the song hit number one stateside and became so popular that it was removed from some jukeboxes to preserve the sanity of waitresses. That song brought the ingredients of the Cuba Libre to a broad audience, but the pedigree of the drink goes back much farther.

HIGHBALL GLASS

2 OUNCES WHITE RUM

5 OUNCES COCA-COLA

LIME JUICE TO TASTE

LIME FOR GARNISH

Build in a highball glass with ice, and stir a few times with a barspoon. Garnish with lime wheel.

★ NOTE ★

Havana Club 3 Year Rum is great for making the Cuba Libre, but you can substitute Caña Brava Rum.

Turn the page for more about the history of the Cuba Libre.

POR CUBA LIBRE

Newspapers owned by William Randolph Hearst and Joseph Pulitzer used the sinking of the USS *Maine* in Havana Harbor in February 1898 to bring the outcry to free Cuba from Spanish rule to a fever pitch. Soldiers gave a U.S. Army post in Jacksonville, Florida, the nickname "Camp Cuba Libre," but the term had existed previously, in a different armed conflict. Freedom fighters during the Ten Years' War often drank hot water sweetened with honey, calling it a Cuba Libre. But there's a good chance that due to differences in translation, "hot water" meant aguardiente. But that still leaves the question of when, where, and how the cola entered the picture.

In 1887, Asa Candler purchased the formula for John Pemberton's tonic made from coca leaves and kola nuts, known now as Coca-Cola. As peace was being negotiated 'tween America and Spain, Candler's brother, Warren, a Methodist bishop, sailed for Cuba to determine what missionary work could be done there and to research opportunities for commercial ventures. After the Treaty of Paris of 1898 ended the war, a Coca-Cola wholesale outfit was established in Havana.

With Coca-Cola's presence entrenched in Havana, the origin story holds that American soldiers at a bar in Cuba, around the time of the Spanish-American War, ordered a rum and Coca-Cola, toasting their Cuban friends: "Por Cuba libre!" From one set of freedom fighters to another, the Cuba Libre as we know it today came to pass.

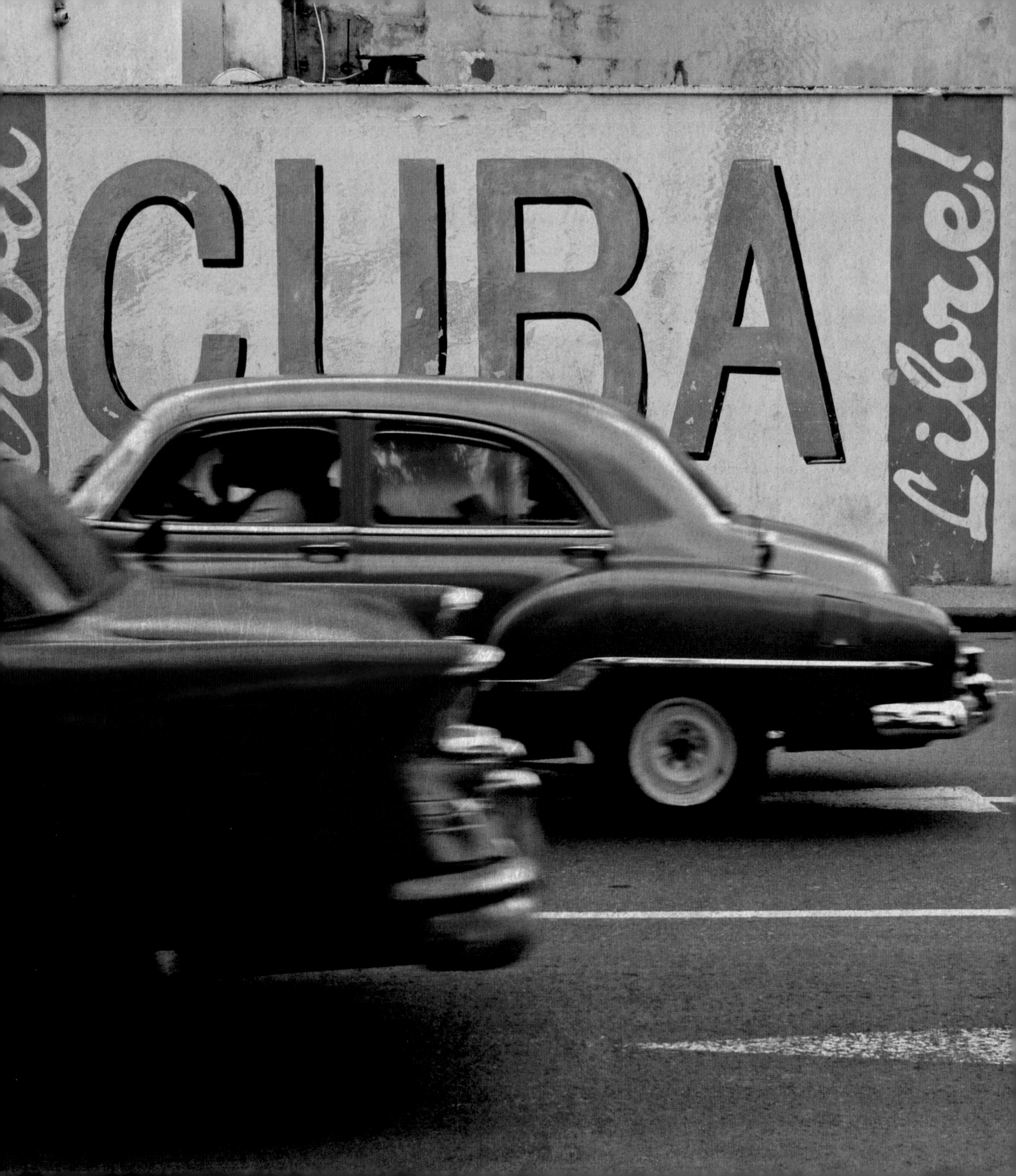
CUBA
Libre!

THE CARIBBEAN

In this modern cocktail, the Cuba Libre gets a modern makeover. This recipe comes from Jeff Berry's *Potions of the Caribbean* and before that hails from a private notebook of Bob Esmino, the bar manager of the Kon-Tiki restaurant chain in Portland, Oregon, Cleveland, and Chicago in the 1960s.

TIKI BOWL

1¼ OUNCES DARK JAMAICAN RUM

1 OUNCE GOLD PUERTO RICAN RUM

½ OUNCE SIMPLE SYRUP (PAGE 10)

¼ OUNCE GINGER SYRUP (PAGE 10)

½ OUNCE LIME JUICE

6 DASHES PERNOD

1 DASH ANGOSTURA BITTERS

1½ OUNCES COCA-COLA

Build all ingredients except the Coca-Cola in a tiki bowl. Swizzle with crushed ice, add Coca-Cola, and swizzle a little more. Serve with a straw.

INTRO TO AWESOME

This cocktail presents our take on Audrey Saunders's Intro to Aperol, which uses gin and, of course, Aperol—a bitter-orange aperitif—as its base. Saunders studied with and worked alongside master mixologist Dale DeGroff in the late 1990s and then opened the Pegu Club in New York City's SoHo neighborhood in August 2005, which helped spark the craft cocktail renaissance. The Intro to Awesome substitutes a dry white rum for the gin to allow the bittersweet notes of the Aperol to shine through. Cucumber works especially well with Aperol, creating an almost watermelon-like flavor.

COLLINS GLASS

6 CUCUMBER SLICES

½ OUNCE SIMPLE SYRUP (PAGE 10)

1½ OUNCES FLOR DE CAÑA EXTRA DRY RUM

1 OUNCE APEROL

1 OUNCE LIME JUICE

1 OUNCE CLUB SODA

SALT FOR GARNISH

In a shaking tin, muddle three cucumber slices in the simple syrup. Build the rest of the drink except club soda. Shake with ice, and double strain into a Collins glass with ice. Top with club soda, a few shakes of salt, and the three remaining cucumber slices.

ISLA TEA

Several origin stories exist for the infamous Long Island Iced Tea. One posits it as the winning entry in a 1972 cocktail competition in which the only stipulation held that the cocktail had to contain triple sec. But references to Long Island Iced Tea exist in Betty Crocker's 1961 *New Picture Cookbook*. Another version holds that the concoction goes as far back as a Prohibition-era drink from Long Island, Tennessee. Either way, Long Island Iced Tea has developed a reputation as the go-to drink for getting smashed fast without tasting any of the ingredients. This modern take provides a balanced cocktail in which you can savor the interaction of the various spirits—instead of just getting bombed at a frat bar.

COLLINS GLASS

½ OUNCE COINTREAU

½ OUNCE CRUZAN BLACK STRAP RUM

½ OUNCE GIN

½ OUNCE MEZCAL

½ OUNCE PLANTATION RUM

½ OUNCE SIMPLE SYRUP (PAGE 10)

½ OUNCE LEMON JUICE

½ OUNCE LIME JUICE

10 DASHES ANGOSTURA BITTERS

1½ OUNCES COCA-COLA

Shake all ingredients except the Coca-Cola with ice. Strain into a Collins glass filled with crushed ice, and top with Coca-Cola.

THE TIKI

& THE COLD WAR

The Cold War transformed the globe into a potential battleground between the USA and the USSR. Nowhere was safe—not even the Caribbean. These drinks deliciously capture the heady anxiety of that time.

TIKI DRINKS

Donn Beachcomber created the tiki family of drinks by amalgamating the experiences of his travels abroad. The style has firm roots in Polynesia, but the base of the cocktails appears in Cuban and other Caribbean classics. Donn Beachcomber called his drinks Rhum Rhapsodies, and many people replicated them, most notably Trader Vic.

In March 1958, Conrad Hilton opened the Habana Hilton, the tallest and largest hotel in the area, which boasted a Trader Vic's bar and restaurant. On January 8, 1959, Castro entered Havana in triumph and made the hotel his headquarters. But that was only the beginning of the tensions between Cuba and U.S. business interests. By October 1960, Castro had completed the nationalization of all American-owned property in Cuba, prompting a retaliatory trade embargo. In April of the following year, the White House sponsored the disastrous Bay of Pigs invasion to topple Castro, who thereafter suspected America of similar plots to overthrow him. In April 1962, the Kennedy administration deployed nuclear missiles to Turkey—within easy striking distance of Moscow. In turn, Soviet premier Nikita Khrushchev accepted Castro's invitation to deploy nuclear missiles to the island nation to act as a deterrent.

As the world teetered on the brink of total annihilation, the exotic allure of tropical drinks grew in parallel with the tensions of the Cold War. Unable to blow off steam safely in the Caribbean, Americans began creating these exotic cocktails in their own backyards.

PIÑA COLADA

Piña colada means "strained pineapple" in Spanish, and Ramon "Monchito" Marrero y Perez reportedly created this version in 1954 at the Caribe Hilton in Puerto Rico. This is the Puerto Rican version of the drink, made possible with the advent of Coco Lopez (page 204).

TIKI BOWL

2 OUNCES WHITE RUM

3 OUNCES COCONUT PUREE

1 OUNCE SIMPLE SYRUP (PAGE 10)

2 OUNCES PINEAPPLE JUICE

½ CUP CRUSHED ICE

PINEAPPLE FOR GARNISH

Combine all ingredients in a blender, and blend for 15 seconds. Pour into a tiki bowl or frozen pineapple shell. Garnish with a pineapple wedge or a cocktail umbrella. For more of a kick, whip shake ingredients and serve over crushed ice.

To make the Cuban version, omit the coconut puree and add ¾ ounce lime juice.

★ NOTE ★

Turn the page for more about the history of the Piña Colada in Cuba.

PIÑA COLADA DE CUBA

Sailors on Christopher Columbus's second voyage to the New World encountered a new fruit that resembled a giant pinecone. They called it a *piña* and brought it back to Europe. Soon after, the pineapple became a symbol of wealth and hospitality.

The original incarnation of El Floridita in Havana was as La Piña de Plata, where the house specialty was pineapple juice. But wherever pineapples grow, they're often combined with rum. Served ice cold, *jugo de piña con ron* (pineapple juice with rum) became fashionable during the tourism explosion that occurred in Cuba after the Spanish-American War. The first written reference to a piña colada comes from a 1922 *Travel* magazine article about "Cuba's Vivacious Metropolis." The author describes this refreshing drink as a mixture of pineapple juice, sugar, rum, and lime juice. Over time, this version has become known as the Cuban Piña Colada, but it continues to evolve. A decade later, in *Bar La Florida Cocktails*, the Havana Beach cocktail consists of pineapple juice, sugar, and rum.

DEMERARA DRY FLOAT

Demerara rums are noted for their dark, smoky, slightly burnt aromas, but the refreshing, tangy passion fruit syrup and nutty, sweet maraschino liqueur in this drink tame the bold rum—before its blazing overproof relative goes to work. Created by Donn Beachcomber around 1941, this lost tiki treasure makes a comeback.

SWIZZLE GLASS

1 OUNCE EL DORADO 5 YEAR RUM

1 TEASPOON MARASCHINO

½ OUNCE PASSION FRUIT SYRUP (PAGE 11)

1 TEASPOON SIMPLE SYRUP (PAGE 10)

1 OUNCE LIME JUICE

HAMILTON 151 RUM TO SERVE

PINEAPPLE FOR GARNISH

Swizzle all ingredients except the 151 in a swizzle glass with crushed ice. Top with 1 barspoon of flaming 151 rum. Garnish with pineapple wedge.

> ★ NOTE ★
>
> *Although it's not a demerara rum, you can also use Gosling's 151, made from molasses.*
>
> *Lemon Hart 151 long was the preferred rum for this recipe. In 1720, Abraham Hart, a German, got into the rumbullion trade in the Caribbean and, with an eye on the market, later relocated to Penzance in Cornwall on the western tip of England. Half a century later, his grandson Lehman "Lemon" Hart joined the family business and for his efforts became the first producer to officially supply the British Royal Navy with the spirit. The rum that bears his name has gone in and out of production, and we hope to see it on shelves again soon.*

DONN BEACHCOMBER

As a child, Ernest Gantt spent winters aboard his grandfather's yacht in the Caribbean, exploring the old bars of Haiti and Havana and taking part in his grandfather's Prohibition-era rum-running. Bootlegging may have been the beginning of Gantt's rum education, but he took it much further. An adventurous spirit lured him around the world a few times and developed his fondness for the romance of the South Pacific.

When Prohibition ended, Gantt opened Don's Beachcomber Café in Hollywood, which he soon renamed Don the Beachcomber Restaurant. (He eventually changed his own name to Donn Beachcomber and later Donn Beach.) The décor was distinctly Polynesian, but the closest thing that the South Pacific had to a mixed drink at that time involved chewing kava root and spitting it into a bowl of coconut milk. Thankfully, Gantt's Caribbean travels guided his beverage program. He amplified the elements, combining base spirits and experimenting with different sweeteners, juices, and methods of incorporating them together. The father of tiki was largely responsible for rum's American comeback. His restaurants alone had used more than 325,000 cases of rum by 1945 and featured rum cellars with 128 expressions from sixteen regions.

The original Don the Beachcomber bar lay on a side street off Hollywood Boulevard, and it was so small that it didn't have its own bathroom; patrons made use of those in the adjoining hotel lobby. But a few days after it opened, Neil Vanderbilt, a roving reporter for the *New York Tribune*, ordered a Sumatra Kula and declared it the "first really good drink I've had for a donkey's year." Thanks to Vanderbilt, Don the Beachcomber was soon teeming with film stars, directors, and producers.

One evening, Marlene Dietrich came in for her favorite tipple, the Beachcomber's Gold. Similar to the Navy Grog (page 199), it featured an elaborate shaved ice garnish. When someone bumped into her, the ice spilled down the plunging neckline of her dress. Donn escorted her to the ladies' lounge of the adjoining hotel, where she yanked down the top of her dress to her waist, saying, "Donn, dry me off quickly!" According to Donn, "Marlene always received pleasure in telling the story whenever the chance permitted. This she did with delight just to see the look it brought to my face."

NAVY GROG

Donn Beachcomber created the Navy Grog during World War II. A large part of the drink's appeal was the garnish of a cone of ice packed around the straw. After the last of the Don the Beachcomber locations closed in the 1980s, this presentation technique was lost until ex-Beachcomber bartender Tony Ramos revealed to Jeff "Beachbum" Berry how to make it. Berry shared the information with Cocktail Kingdom, where today you can buy the mold for all your Navy Grog garnishing needs.

ROCKS GLASS

1 OUNCE EL DORADO 8 YEAR RUM

½ OUNCE BANKS FIVE ISLAND RUM

¾ OUNCE HONEY SYRUP (PAGE 11)

¼ OUNCE CINNAMON SYRUP (PAGE 10)

¾ OUNCE GRAPEFRUIT JUICE

¾ OUNCE LIME JUICE

ANGOSTURA BITTERS

Whip shake all ingredients except the bitters, and pour into a large chilled rocks glass. Top with crushed ice, a grog cone of ice, and bitters to taste. Serve with a straw.

"Don't talk to me about naval tradition. It's nothing but rum, sodomy, and the lash."

—ATTRIBUTED TO WINSTON CHURCHILL

TIKI BOWL

Tiki bowls take their inspiration from aboriginal Polynesian kava bowls used for ceremonial occasions. The bowls range from 12 to 30 inches in diameter and have short legs. A cleaned and polished coconut shell served as a cup for distributing the ceremonial beverage for everyone. Created by Trader Vic circa 1950, this is one of his numerous communal drinks, meant to be shared.

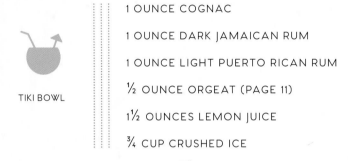

TIKI BOWL

1 OUNCE COGNAC

1 OUNCE DARK JAMAICAN RUM

1 OUNCE LIGHT PUERTO RICAN RUM

½ OUNCE ORGEAT (PAGE 11)

1½ OUNCES LEMON JUICE

¾ CUP CRUSHED ICE

Blend at high speed for 10 seconds. Pour into a tiki bowl for two.

For more kick and eye-catching presentation, whip shake the liquid ingredients, and serve over crushed ice. Then fill a lime shell with overproof rum, and set it ablaze!

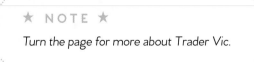

★ NOTE ★

Turn the page for more about Trader Vic.

TRADER VIC

Victor Bergeron had a tough start in life, losing a leg and a kidney
to tuberculosis. Unable to finish school or hold down a job
because of his health, he eventually started working at his uncle's
saloon, using his charm and wits to mask his lack of experience
as a bartender.

After a fallout with his uncle, he opened his own place, Hinky
Dinks, across the street. It was the middle of the Great Depression,
and Vic realized the value of the escapist nature of hospitality: His
customers couldn't necessarily afford to spend the money they
were spending, but a need to retreat from the harsh realities of
everyday life brought them to Hinky Dinks. Vic worked to give
his venue a distinctive atmosphere, going for an Alaskan hunting
lodge vibe first.

A trip to Los Angeles brought him to Don the Beachcomber,
the hottest spot in town. It had not only an exotic atmosphere
but exotic cocktails as well. Vic suggested to Donn that they
collaborate—to no avail. Deciding to do Don the Beachcomber
one better, Vic and his wife headed to the Caribbean in 1938. In
Havana, Vic met Constantino Ribalaigua i Vert, his future mentor.

Vic watched and learned and in his autobiography gives full credit to El Constante for teaching him how to make tropical drinks.

Twenty years and about twenty-five Trader Vic's locations later, Vic returned to the site where he had first learned to make daiquirís from the master … but he didn't stay long. Relations between Cuba and America deteriorated into the trade embargo. Cuban rum and cocktails, once a pillar of the American cocktail palate, became unattainable, but the tiki trend continued.

CARIBE WELCOME

Before the piña colada replaced it, this was the signature drink at the Caribe Hilton. Until the mid-1950s, rendering coconut cream was a long and arduous process. Before then it involved sourcing young coconuts, draining the coconut water from them, hacking them open, prying the white flesh from the shells, hand-grinding the flesh to cream it, and then whipping it. Nowadays we would use a food processor, but it's still easier to buy than make. In 1954, a professor at the University of Puerto Rico automated the process, producing Coco Lopez Coconut Cream, and personally approached chefs and bartenders to encourage them to experiment with his new product. Thanks to the pioneering work of Ramon Lopez y Irizarry, we can enjoy this beverage without having to crack a bunch of coconuts.

COCONUT SHELL

1½ OUNCES GOLD PUERTO RICAN RUM

½ OUNCE APRICOT BRANDY

2 OUNCES COCONUT WATER

½ OUNCE COCO LOPEZ COCONUT CREAM

3 TEASPOONS LIME JUICE

Shake all ingredients over ice. Pour, unstrained, into a coconut shell.

SIBONEY

The Siboney were a native people who lived in the western part of Cuba, pushed there and beyond to Hispaniola by the Taíno people, the main indigenous group of people on Cuba. By around 1600, all the Siboney had died, but their memory lives on. Today, Siboney is a small town and beach near Santiago de Cuba. Ernesto Lecuano used the name for a 1929 song that he wrote about his homesickness when he was away from Cuba. The song quickly became a Cuban classic, and Bing Crosby sang an English version. This recipe, which comes from Trader Vic's 1974 book *Rum Cookery & Drinkery*, captures some of the bittersweet longing of the song.

TIKI BOWL

1 OUNCE DARK JAMAICAN RUM

½ OUNCE PASSION FRUIT SYRUP (PAGE 11)

½ OUNCE LEMON JUICE

½ OUNCE UNSWEETENED PINEAPPLE JUICE

Shake all ingredients over ice, and strain into a small tiki bowl.

MISSIONARY'S DOWNFALL

Another Don the Beachcomber original, this recipe hails from the family of Hank Riddle, who worked at several Don the Beachcomber restaurants from the 1940s to the 1980s, according to Jeff Berry in *Beachbum Berry Remixed*. This frozen tiki treat has the perfect blend of fruit, herbs, sweetness, and acidity—but it packs a punch. As the name suggests, one too many of this delicious drink might prove to be your downfall.

BEER GLASS

2 OUNCES WHITE RUM

½ OUNCE PEACH BRANDY

½ OUNCE HONEY SYRUP (PAGE 11)

1 OUNCE LIME JUICE

4 PINEAPPLE WEDGES (RINDS REMOVED)

6 MINT LEAVES, PLUS EXTRA FOR GARNISH

1 CUP CRUSHED ICE

PINEAPPLE FOR GARNISH

Blend all ingredients, and pour, unstrained, into a beer glass. Garnish lavishly with mint sprigs and pineapple wedge.

ANCIENT MARINER

According to Jeff Berry, the Ancient Mariner is an attempt to re-create the flavors of Trader Vic's Navy Grog, which was itself an attempt to decipher Don the Beachcomber's drink of the same name (page 199). Berry created this version, which appeared in his *Grog Log*.

TIKI BOWL

1 OUNCE APPLETON ESTATE RESERVE RUM

1 OUNCE EL DORADO 12 YEAR RUM

½ OUNCE VANILLA SYRUP (PAGE 11)

¾ OUNCE LIME JUICE

½ OUNCE GRAPEFRUIT JUICE

¼ OUNCE ST. ELIZABETH ALLSPICE DRAM

GRAPEFRUIT FOR GARNISH

Whip shake all ingredients, and strain into a tiki bowl filled with crushed ice. Garnish with a grapefruit wedge.

The ice was here, the ice was there,

The ice was all around:

It cracked and growled, and roared and howled,

Like noises in a swound!

—SAMUEL TAYLOR COLERIDGE,
FROM "THE RIME OF THE ANCIENT MARINER" (1834)

SOL Y SOMBRA

Egyptian-born Joe Scialom created this drink after becoming the bar manager at the Caribe Hilton. He later became the beverage superintendent at the Havana Hilton. During his time in the Caribbean, he proclaimed rum to be "the best mixer"—high praise from a man who was at one point Cuba's most famous bartender. The name means "sun and shadow" in Spanish, and this recipe comes to us from *Potions of the Caribbean* by Jeff "Beachbum" Berry, who located it in Joe Scialom's private papers.

PINEAPPLE SHELL

1½ OUNCES GOLD PUERTO RICAN RUM

¾ OUNCE DARK JAMAICAN RUM

½ OUNCE APRICOT BRANDY

2 OUNCES PINEAPPLE JUICE

½ OUNCE LIME JUICE

2 DASHES ANGOSTURA BITTERS

PINEAPPLE SHELL FOR SERVING

Shake all ingredients over ice. Pour, unstrained, into a hollowed-out pineapple. Serve with an umbrella.

Cocteles Cubanos includes a totally different recipe that features the same name:

15 ML AGED RUM

30 ML CRÈME DE CACAO

Build in a glass, and serve with a glass of water.

This Sol y Sombra is attributed to José Maria Vazquez, the bartender at the Hotel Lincoln, who created the Mulata Daiquirí (page 136). It was entered in the first cocktail contest held by the Club de Cantineros, where it won an award.

ZOMBIE

Donn Beachcomber infamously instructed of this cocktail: "only two to a customer." The original recipe remained a mystery until Jeff "Beachbum" Berry uncovered it in a notebook belonging to Beachcomber's headwaiter Dick Santiago.

COLLINS GLASS

1 OUNCE BARBANCOURT 4 YEAR RUM

1 OUNCE EL DORADO 3 YEAR RUM

½ OUNCE APPLETON V/X RUM

½ OUNCE CORUBA JAMAICAN RUM

½ OUNCE CURAÇAO

½ OUNCE EL DORADO 151 RUM

½ OUNCE PASSION FRUIT SYRUP (PAGE 11)

¼ OUNCE CINNAMON SYRUP (PAGE 10)

¼ OUNCE ORGEAT (PAGE 11)

1 OUNCE LIME JUICE

¾ OUNCE GRAPEFRUIT JUICE

4 DASHES ABSINTHE

4 DASHES ANGOSTURA BITTERS

4 DASHES MARASCHINO

PINEAPPLE, LIME, GRAPEFRUIT, MINT, AND SEASONAL BERRIES FOR GARNISH

Build in a shaking tin, and dry shake. Pour over crushed ice, and garnish with pineapple, lime, grapefruit, mint sprigs, and berries.

Turn the page for more about the genesis of the Zombie.

ZOMBIE

Donn Beachcomber created the Zombie for a friend on his way to the airport who wanted a "tall, cool one" before a flight to San Francisco. Donn mixed five different rums with other ingredients and served it to his friend. The drink went down so well that the friend asked for two more. A few days later, the friend returned, wanting to know what was in that drink. It turns out that after consuming three of them, he got into a fight with his driver, got into an argument on the airplane, and later found himself seated on a San Francisco dock, his feet dangling over the side. The Zombie got its name and its two-drink maximum because the friend felt "like the walking dead."

The two-Zombie maximum was tested one more time by a local mobster. When the bartender refused the man a third order, the mobster bet Donn one hundred dollars that he could handle at least five without any problems. Beach matched his wager: One hundred dollars said he couldn't finish even three. A few days later, the man returned to the bar. Beach and the mobster each handed one hundred dollars to the bartender. The mobster drank two Zombies, but halfway through the third his head hit the

— MEA HOOMANAO—"A thing to remember"—

bar—a knockout. Donn took his winnings and warned the mobster's companions, "Always remember the Beachcomber's Rule Number Two: Never bet on another man's game."

Donn neglected to mention that he had laced the Zombies with glycerin to make sure the mobster never stood a chance.

THE MODERN

& THE FUTURE

Our friends and family
created these drinks
with Cuba on their mind.

CONTEMPORARY INTERPRETATIONS

Our trip to Cuba found cocktail culture alive and well. Beverage tourism is obvious, but if you look carefully you can spot quiet hints of backlash; one privately owned bar proudly brags, "HEMINGWAY NEVER DRANK HERE." Cuba has a long, rewarding history of making do. Despite limited access to ingredients, bartenders have a strong knowledge of their trade and its history, which they use to create menus that boast a deep collection of classics while keeping an eye on the future. Our friends and family in the industry, who make some of the best drinks around, do the same. Here are some of their Cuban-inspired cocktails.

PATTER FLASH

Jessica Wholers

Patter flash was a slang language used by thieves and pickpockets in the nineteenth century. Jessica took her inspiration for the name of this cocktail from Stolen Spiced Rum, which in turn was inspired by Jim Jarmusch's movie *Coffee and Cigarettes*. The rum is blended with fenugreek from Morocco, vanilla bean from Madagascar, and Arabica coffee beans from Colombia, creating an atmospheric liqueur full of smoke and coffee notes. Solbeso is a liqueur distilled from cacao fruit.

ROCKS GLASS

2 OUNCES STOLEN SPICED RUM

¾ OUNCE SOLBESO

1 BARSPOON VANILLA SYRUP (PAGE 11)

1 DASH ANGOSTURA BITTERS

Stir all ingredients over ice, and strain into a rocks glass with ice.

"Cigarettes and coffee, man, that's the combination."

—IGGY POP, IN *COFFEE AND CIGARETTES*

TESTAROSSA COLLINS

Tom Chadwick

French house musician Kavinsky inspired Tom Chadwick of Cienfuegos and Dram Bar to make this riff on a Collins. Kavinsky's storyline is that he crashed his Ferrari Testarossa in 1986 and then mysteriously came back to life as a zombie. The Italian luxury car in the story appears in the drink in the form of Fernet Branca, a stylish Italian amaro.

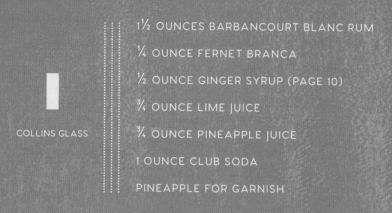

COLLINS GLASS

1½ OUNCES BARBANCOURT BLANC RUM

¼ OUNCE FERNET BRANCA

½ OUNCE GINGER SYRUP (PAGE 10)

¾ OUNCE LIME JUICE

¾ OUNCE PINEAPPLE JUICE

1 OUNCE CLUB SODA

PINEAPPLE FOR GARNISH

Build all ingredients except club soda in a shaking tin. Shake, and strain into a Collins glass filled with ice. Top with club soda, garnish with a pineapple wedge, and serve with a straw.

THE KEENAN

Anne Robinson

Head bartender at Little Park and Evening Bar in New York City's Smyth Hotel, Anne Robinson is no stranger to the ways of a black strap daiquirí. Here she dresses it up by fortifying it with rich Tempus Fugit and the dry and spicy allspice dram. Together they tame the bodacious black strap into a delectable quaff.

COUPE

2 OUNCES CRUZAN BLACK STRAP RUM

⅜ OUNCE TEMPUS FUGIT CRÈME DE CACAO

½ OUNCE SIMPLE SYRUP (PAGE 10)

1 OUNCE LIME JUICE

3 DASHES ST. ELIZABETH ALLSPICE DRAM

LIME FOR GARNISH

Build all ingredients except allspice dram in shaking tin, and shake. Strain into a chilled coupe rinsed with the allspice dram. Garnish with a lime wheel.

★ NOTE ★

Black strap rum is rum made with the addition of black strap molasses, the result of the third boiling of sugar syrup.

COBRA'S FANG

Brian Miller

Based on the 1937 Don the Beachcomber drink of the same name, this cocktail comes to us from the Tiki Monday Crew, the popup bar by Brian Miller, one of the original bartenders at Death & Co. It's a classic made modern by using Hamilton 151 Rum from Guyana.

ROCKS GLASS

1½ OUNCES HAMILTON 151 RUM

½ OUNCE VELVET FALERNUM

½ OUNCE PASSION FRUIT PUREE

½ OUNCE CINNAMON SYRUP (PAGE 10)

¾ OUNCE LIME JUICE

½ OUNCE ORANGE JUICE

2 DASHES ABSINTHE

1 DASH ANGOSTURA BITTERS

CINNAMON FOR GARNISH

Shake with 3 ice cubes. Strain into a double rocks glass with crushed ice. Grate fresh cinnamon over the top, and garnish with a cinnamon stick. Serve with a straw.

★ NOTE ★

Velvet Falernum is a must-have rum-based liqueur flavored with almonds, cloves, ginger, lime zest, and other spices.

THE IMPROVED

Sother Teague

Head bartender at Amor y Amargo—a bitters tasting room and New York City's only bitters-focused bar—Sother Teague regularly serves this deliciously astringent cocktail, which is a variation of the Kingston Negroni by Joaquin Simo, owner of Pouring Ribbons and one of the first bartenders at Death & Co. This recipe favors a less funky Barbadian (Bajan for short) rum as the base and adds zucca, a rhubarb-based Italian amaro, to smooth the edges.

ROCKS GLASS

1¼ OUNCES COCKSPUR 12 YEAR RUM

¾ OUNCE ANTICA CARPANO SWEET VERMOUTH

¾ OUNCE ZUCCA

¼ OUNCE SMITH & CROSS RUM

10 DROPS BITTERMENS TIKI BITTERS

ORANGE FOR GARNISH

Build in a mixing glass, stir briefly, and pour into a double rocks glass with a large piece of ice. Garnish with an orange twist.

★ NOTE ★

Avery and Janet Glasser make their 'Elemakule Tiki Bitters in New Orleans. Featuring strong cinnamon and allspice flavors, they took their inspiration from Brian Miller (page 223), who asked if they ever thought about making Falernum, a cordial.

CRADLE OF LIFE

Karin Stanley

"Flavors that are at once exotic and familiar" is the tag line for this Scorpion Bowl–inspired tiki drink, a house classic from Dutch Kills Bar in the Long Island City neighborhood of New York City. Tiki cocktails often combine two or more rums to give depth and control to the overall balance of the cocktail.

ROCKS GLASS

¾ OUNCE AGED RUM

¾ OUNCE SPICED RUM

½ OUNCE ORGEAT (PAGE 11)

⅜ OUNCE LEMON JUICE

⅜ OUNCE LIME JUICE

⅜ OUNCE ORANGE JUICE

2 DASHES ANGOSTURA BITTERS

½ OUNCE GREEN CHARTREUSE

Combine all ingredients except Chartreuse in a shaker, and dry shake. Pour into a chilled double rocks glass, and top with crushed ice and an inverted lime half. Add Chartreuse to the inverted lime half, light it on fire, and serve.

★ NOTE ★

For an inverted lime half, cut a lime in half, squeeze out the juice, and use a bottle to press it inside out. Clean off any excess pulp with a dry towel.

UNCLE WINSTON'S JAMAICAN SENSATION

Mayur Subbarao

"Mayur Subbarao is a serious drinker" began a *New York Times* article on New York City's cocktail brotherhood in 2008. Subbarao knows his way around both sides of the bar, and he created this cocktail when mai tais were on his mind. He transformed the Polynesian classic with the addition of gin, which gets the Jamaican rum spinning—which we think is sensational!

ROCKS GLASS

¾ OUNCE APPLETON ESTATE V/X RUM

¾ OUNCE BEEFEATER GIN

¼ OUNCE ORANGE CURAÇAO

¾ OUNCE ORGEAT (PAGE 11)

¾ OUNCE LIME JUICE

¼ OUNCE PINEAPPLE JUICE

MINT FOR GARNISH

Build all ingredients in shaking tin, whip shake, and pour into a double rocks glass. Top with crushed ice, garnish with mint sprigs, and serve with a straw.

THE COLONIAL

Frank Cisneros

Coffee and rum have always had a natural affinity for each other. The *carajillo* is a Spanish coffee cocktail typically made with brandy or whiskey. In Cuba, it's made—of course—with rum. It dates back to the Spanish occupation of the island when soldiers added rum to their coffee for a little extra courage. This cocktail follows the long tradition of liquid courage but is better as an after-dinner drink rather than a pre-battle pick-me-up.

COUPE

1½ OUNCES BANKS FIVE ISLAND RUM

1¼ OUNCES COLD BREWED COFFEE

½ OUNCE CHINATO COCCHI

1 BARSPOON FARETTI BISCOTTI LIQUEUR OR AMARETTO

1 DROP ROSE WATER

1 BARSPOON YELLOW CHARTREUSE

GRAPEFRUIT FOR GARNISH

Build the first five ingredients in a mixing glass, and stir. Strain into a chilled coupe rinsed with Chartreuse. Twist grapefruit peel over the top to release the oils, and discard.

"Went to bed about two o'clock in the afternoon, stupidly drunk."

—NICHOLAS CRESWELL,
A BRITISH TRAVELER IN THE NORTH AMERICAN COLONIES,
JANUARY 7, 1776

IMAGE CREDITS

FURTHER READING

Berry, Jeff. *Beachbum Berry's Potions of the Caribbean*. New York: Cocktail Kingdom, 2003.

Bitner, Arnold. *Scrounging the Islands with the Legendary Don the Beachcomber: Host to Diplomat, Beachcomber, Prince and Pirate*. Lincoln, NE: iUniverse, 2007.

Bolton, Ross. *Bar La Florida Cocktails* (1935 reprint). Charleston, SC: CreateSpace, 2008.

Broom, Dave. *Rum*. South San Francisco, CA: Wine Appreciation Guild, 2003.

Curtis, Wayne. *And a Bottle of Rum: A History of the New World in Ten Cocktails*. New York: Crown Publishers, 2006.

English, T. J. *Havana Nocturne: How the Mob Owned Cuba . . . and Then Lost It to the Revolution*. New York: William Morrow, 2008.

Fiedler, Jennifer. *The Essential Bar Book: An A-to-Z Guide to Spirits, Cocktails, and Wine with 115 Recipes for the World's Great Drinks*. Berkeley, CA: Ten Speed Press, 2014.

Foss, Richard. *Rum: A Global History*. London: Reaktion Books, 2012.

Gjelten, Tom. *Bacardi and the Long Fight for Cuba: The Biography of a Cause*. New York: Viking, 2008.

Miller, Anistatia, and Jared Brown. *Cuban Cocktails: Drinks and the Cantineros behind Them from Cuba's Golden Age*. Cheltenham, Gloucestershire, UK: Mixellany, 2012.

Regan, Gary. *The Joy of Mixology*. New York: Clarkson Potter, 2003.

RECIPE INDEX

GENERAL INDEX